ACTING
IN YOUNG
HOLLYWOOD

ACTING
IN YOUNG
HOLLYWOOD

A CAREER GUIDE FOR KIDS, TEENS, AND ADULTS WHO PLAY YOUNG, TOO

FREDERICK LEVY

WATSON-GUPTILL PUBLICATIONS / NEW YORK

Copyright © 2009 by Management 101, Inc.

First published in 2009 by Back Stage Books
an imprint of Crown Publishing Group, a division of Random House Inc., New York
www.crownpublishing.com
www.watsonguptill.com

BACK STAGE is a registered trademark of Nielsen Business Media, Inc.

Library of Congress Control Number: 2009925808
ISBN: 978-0-8230-8955-0

Designed by
Dominika Dmytrowski

Printed in the United States

First printing, 2009

1 2 3 4 5 6 7 8 9 / 15 14 13 12 11 10 09

FOR MY CLIENTS,
WHO INSPIRE AND IMPRESS ME
AND MAKE ME LOVE WHAT I DO.

AND FOR BRYAN LEDER:
"IT'S THE LEAST THAT I COULD DO."

TABLE OF CONTENTS

ACKNOWLEDGMENTS

I'd like to thank my agent, Andree Abecassis of the Ann Elmo Agency, who unknowingly has taught me a thing or two about being a good rep. I'd also like to thank Amy Vinchesi at Watson-Guptill for believing in me and this book, and Gary Sunshine for his excellent job editing this manuscript.

A special thank-you to my clients and colleagues who allowed me to interview them for this book: Carey Arban, Austin Basis, Lauren Bass, Mike Beaty, Tanya Berezin, Melissa Berger, Nathan Biay, Jenni Blong, Abby Bluestone, Asher Book, Hartford Brown, Andrew Caldwell, Jodi Caldwell, Colin Fickes, Julie Fulop, Kate Godard, Angie Grant, Harriet Greenspan, Shane Harper, Tanya Harper, Vivian Hollander, James Immekus, Leza Labrador, Dennis LaValle, Philip Leader, Bryan Leder, Michelle Lewitt, Jamie Malone, Nancy Mancuso, Rocky Marquette, Ben McKenzie, Blaine Miller, Mary Mouser, Tina Mouser, Ian Nelson, Susan Osser, Scott Plimpton, Carla Renata, Dianne Samonas, Judy Savage, and Ron Scott.

A special thank-you to Hema Kathireson for her help with research. I'd also like to thank the entire staff at Management 101 that helps make our company so special.

Shout-outs to Hilary Cherniss, Melissa Wurster, Wesley Eure, Rick Joyce, Andy Puschoegl, Andrew Friedman, Joby Harte, cousin Roberta Gold, my parents Barry and Lois Levy, my brother David Levy, and all of my friends and family who encourage and support me.

PREFACE

In 2000, when I wrote my first book, *Hollywood 101: The Film Industry*, I left out a very important aspect of the entertainment business: acting. This wasn't because I didn't feel acting was important; rather, there was so much to say on the subject that I felt it needed its own volume to truly do it justice. However, I was in no position to write that book back then.

Shortly after the book was published, I began receiving letters and e-mails from readers all around the world. "Dear Frederick, Thank you for writing this book. It changed my life. I'm packing up my truck, I'm moving to L.A., and I finally have a game plan on how to pursue my Hollywood dreams." I was humbled. I could not believe my words had affected so many lives. I began to ponder if I was doing what I should be doing with my own professional career.

For several years, I had been the vice president of development at Marty Katz Productions, the production company responsible for such films as *Reindeer Games* and *The Four Feathers*. But I felt it was time for a change, and I began to explore other opportunities. The most intriguing to me was an offer to work at a management firm, helping them start a division that would produce film and television projects for their clients. Subconsciously, I thought working at a management firm might place me in an environment where I could continue helping people break into and succeed in their entertainment careers, just as I had done with my writing. So I asked them to teach me the management business. They agreed.

At first I was just going to represent writers because, coming from a production and development background, that's really what I knew. But a friend of mine who was an actor had always told me, "If you ever become a *manager*, I want you to manage me." So I called her up and said, "I'm a manager. Would you like to be my first client? If it works, great. But if it doesn't, let's still be friends."

Somehow, it worked. What's more, I quickly began having fun, and we started to have great success. I was dividing my time between management and production, but I was soon becoming enamored of my role as a manager. I truly enjoyed the personal interaction with clients and seeing the immediate results of my efforts.

The management firm where I first worked primarily represented adults. Taye Diggs, Adam Rodriguez, and David McCallum were some of our clients. Then one day I got a call from my cousin Roberta who lived in Fredericksburg, Virginia.

"I just saw the most amazing kid in the local dinner theater production of *Oliver!*. He now lives in L.A., and you should meet him," said Roberta.

"I don't rep kids," I told her.

But she was fairly insistent. "Just meet with him. He's got a great family and he's out in L.A. and they could use some advice."

So I met with this kid and his family. He was just twelve years old and he'd been living full-time in Los Angeles for the last year with family friends. His mom was a flight attendant who flew back and forth from Virginia to L.A. biweekly. Once a month, he would fly home to visit his dad and brother.

At twelve years old, he took a great meeting. I was impressed with his story and how he presented himself in a room. They left me with a tape of his *Oliver!* performance, which I watched that evening. It, too, was remarkable.

The next day I asked one of my colleagues why we didn't represent children.

"There's no money in kids," he said.

Sure there might not be as much money at first, I thought, but eventually these kids grow up and potentially continue to book jobs. "If I can help build a career from the ground up, won't it be all the more fulfilling when they reach the top?" I asked.

"Do whatever you want," he said. "But they can be a lot more trouble than they're worth. And the parents . . . don't even get me started."

I decided to take a chance. Blaine Miller was a talented kid who was clearly dedicated to succeeding in this business. At just twelve years old he had already sacrificed so much just to be in Los Angeles and give it a go. His parents seemed normal and supportive. And I decided to take him on as a client. Working with Blaine paid off immediately as the young actor became a booking machine, landing recurring roles on shows like *Reno 911, Jack & Bobby,* and *Ned's Declassified School Survival Guide*. In addition, he has booked dozens of **guest star** roles in television, supporting roles in movies, national commercials, and live stage shows. He even booked a **series regular** gig as one of the stars of Disney Channel's *Movie Surfers.*

What I learned from Blaine is that I love working with kids and teens. I have a gift for developing talent and helping to launch their careers. With Blaine's success, I started signing more young actors. Eventually I realized I wanted to focus all of my attention on managing actors, rather than producing projects for my colleagues' clients. So I left that firm.

I started my company, Management 101, the very next day. When people ask me the best part of what I do, I say without hesitation, "Helping an actor get their first job." It's always an amazing accomplishment, no matter how big or small that job is. It creates an indescribable feeling of excitement and pride, for both the client and me.

My company has grown and flourished over the years, and I am now a top talent manager actively working in the business. No, I don't represent Brad Pitt and Julia Roberts; rather, I specialize in developing fresh new talent. While I work with talent of all ages, I focus primarily on the *youth market*. My clients can be seen on shows like *Hannah Montana*, *The Suite Life of Zack & Cody*, and *iCarly*, as well as in movies like *Transformers, Bratz: The Movie*, and *Fame*.

We've got a solid reputation and a client roster of talented working actors who are quickly becoming stars before my very eyes. Having shepherded this company from the beginning, I can't think of any other research that would have made me better equipped to write this book.

I've wanted to write *Acting in Young Hollywood* for a long time now. Every time I attend a talent convention, or speak in an acting class, I get the same questions thrown at me. Finally, I have a book to share with actors and parents of young performers everywhere that will help answer their questions and give them a leg up on navigating the entertainment industry.

While this is a fun business, it's also very competitive and a lot of work. But I've always believed if you dream it, you can make it happen. I hope the information contained herein will help you achieve your dreams.

THE YOUTH GENERATION

Hannah Montana. High School Musical. iCarly. The youth market is taking Hollywood by storm. As such, there's never been a better time for aspiring kid and teen actors to break into show business. And for those young actors who already have a foot in the door, now is the time to capitalize on the success of this youth revolution and take your career to the next level.

But the youth market includes more than kids and teens. In today's entertainment industry, thirty is the new twenty, and as long as you look and play younger than you are, you could be a part of young Hollywood also. And, like kids and teens, you could also be highly in demand.

This Is Our Youth

As our clients at Management 101 grow older, some move on to adult roles while others hold onto their youthful looks and continue to play characters that are much younger than the actors truly are. For the purposes of this book, I have defined the youth market as anyone under eighteen, or anyone over eighteen who plays under eighteen.

Of course, if you are over eighteen, you must be realistic about the age range you play. Some actors, like Jason Earles, the thirty-two-year-old man who plays Jackson Stewart, the teenage brother of Miley Stewart on Disney Channel's hit series *Hannah Montana*, looks like a real teen. But not every thirty-two-year-old can pull that off.

Sometimes **producers** choose to cast everyone older, so it doesn't matter if an actor truly looks like a teen as long as every other actor on the show appears to be the same age. Take the original *Beverly Hills, 90210*, for instance. Luke Perry was twenty-five when he took on the role of teenage bad boy Dylan McKay. But because most of the other actors playing teens on that show were also older, producers were able to get away with it.

You're probably thinking, why would producers want to cast older actors to play younger? Wouldn't they want to keep things more realistic? The answer is simple: An adult can work more hours than a child. And the older the child, the more hours he can work. We'll go into the specifics of child labor laws later on, in chapter 10.

In the meantime, suffice it to say, the older you are, and the younger you can play, the more opportunities will come your way. This doesn't always bode well for young people who look older than they really are. In fact, teenage girls have a particularly difficult time finding work once they go through puberty. While they may look all grown up, they can't work as many hours as an actual adult. So they're too old to play children and too costly to be hired for the older roles when there's someone who is eighteen or older who can easily play the part.

"At some point, know you will catch up and look your age," sympathizes Jamie Malone, a manager and owner of MC Talent. "The best advice is don't try to look older. If you're tall, don't wear heels. If you're busty, invest in a minimizer bra. Don't wear things that accentuate your curves."

It's one thing to look older naturally, but it's a whole other ballgame when you make yourself look older with makeup and clothes. And, not to pick on the girls, but this pertains mostly to them. Dress your age . . . or younger. If Dad wouldn't want you wearing a particular outfit to school, then you probably shouldn't be wearing it to *auditions*. Low-cut blouses and hiked-up skirts will only make you look older, and in a business where youth is currency, you're short-changing your career.

Likewise, clean faces are key. Most kids do not wear makeup, and neither should you. If you think you need to apply makeup to make you look younger, then chances are you've moved beyond the youth market.

"Girls need to learn to work with what they've got by not adding any component such as makeup that would make them look even more mature," notes Julie Fulop, a commercial and *theatrical agent* with AKA. "They need to look at the age of the character they are reading for and incorporate that into their makeup choices."

"Makeup should only enhance your beauty, not cover it up or distract," adds Malone. "Less is more. A little mascara is all you need. Blend in skin flaws with a natural product. Stay away from heavy eyeliner."

If things are slow because of how you look at a certain age, then take this time to work on your craft. "Youth and innocence has to come from within, so if you already look older than you really are, then you need to study and do some coaching on *being* youthful," says Michelle Lewitt, a **casting director** with the Casting Company. "Alison Lohman played a fourteen-year-old when she was close to twenty-two, I believe. Yes, she looked young, but if she didn't have the acting chops to actually pull off a fourteen-year-old's demeanor, she wouldn't have been cast no matter how young she looked."

Employers

Sure there's work for kids and teens all over the five-hundred-channel dial, not to mention films, commercials, and live stage jobs. But there are a few companies that dominate the youth market providing a significant amount of employment opportunities for young actors. We'll discuss these major youth networks, alphabetically, below.

ABC Family is geared toward teens, and their programming skews to a female audience. Shows like *Kyle XY, Greek,* and *The Secret Life of the American Teenager* have put them on the map. They're also known for their original movies like *Bring It On: All or Nothing, Samurai Girl,* and *The Cutting Edge 3: Chasing the Dream.*

Cartoon Network carries mostly animated programming—but don't let that fool you. Actors are needed to voice all the characters in each show. Some of their animated fare includes *Ben 10: Alien Force, Star Wars: The Clone Wars,* and *Chowder*. Recently, they've also begun to include live-action programming on the network. Their first live-action series is called *Out of Jimmy's Head*. Live-action movies include *Ben 10: Race Against Time, Re-Animated,* and *Scooby Doo: In the Beginning*.

Disney Channel has transformed itself into a major powerhouse in the tween market. Creating stars is what they do best, and their network roster reads like a who's who of teen magazine cover models. Shows include *Hannah Montana, The Suite Life on Deck,* and *Wizards of Waverly Place*. Their original movies include *Camp Rock* and the *High School Musical* franchise.

Disney XD is a newer spin-off channel from Disney Channel that is aimed specifically at boys. Previously, this slot on the dial was occupied by the now-defunct Toon Disney. Live-action shows include *Aaron Stone* and *Zeke & Luther*. Animated entries include *Phineas and Ferb* and *Batman: The Animated Series*.

MTV is worth mentioning here only because it is geared toward an older teen demographic and its shows like *The Hills* and *America's Best Dance Crew* continue to draw big numbers. However, at this time, most of their programming is non-scripted with the exception of an occasional original movie like *The American Mall*.

Nickelodeon is Disney's fiercest competitor for the tween market. They've got a large presence in both Los Angeles and New York. Their shows include *iCarly, The Naked Brothers Band,* and *True Jackson VP.* Their original movies include *Gym Teacher: The Movie* and *Shredderman Rules!* They've also got a stronghold in animation with shows like *SpongeBob Squarepants.*

The CW definitely targets older teens. Their edgy programming includes soaps like *Gossip Girl, One Tree Hill,* and the new *90210.* They're also known for their sci-fi fare with shows like *Smallville* and *Supernatural.*

The N is Nickelodeon's response to ABC Family. However, most of their programming is imported from Canada, including shows like *Degrassi: The Next Generation* and *Instant Star.* They do have some original programming as well, and they're not afraid to push the envelope. Just watch *South of Nowhere.*

Variety

They say that variety is the spice of life. That adage has never rung truer than in today's Hollywood, especially when it comes to the youth market. More than ever, networks and studios strive to promote diversity in the projects they make and in their casting choices.

Diversity comes in many different forms. It goes far beyond race and gender to include culture, body type, and sexual orientation. No matter where you fit in the mix, opportunities abound for you on the silver screen.

Many of the major networks have diversity initiatives. Some, like CBS and ABC, have annual showcases where minority actors are given an opportunity to perform scenes in front of the professional casting community. Other companies are developing projects specifically for, or to include roles for, under-represented groups.

No one is more in the forefront of the diversity movement than the youth networks. Just look at a project like Disney Channel's original movie *The Cheetah Girls One World*. The film's stars are Adrienne Bailon, who has Ecuadorian and Puerto Rican roots; African American actress Kiely Williams; and Sabrina Bryan, who is a biracial mix of Mexican and Caucasian. Aspiring actors who look at the TV screen can feel certain, regardless of your background, there is a place for you.

Ever-Changing Market

The landscape of the youth market is ever changing. The talent pool is constantly growing older, and fresh, new actors are constantly entering the gate. But the players are continually changing as well.

When I was a kid, PBS was the only children's network around. Child and teen stars dominated the major networks in family shows like *The Facts of Life*, *Growing Pains*, and *Life Goes On*. Nickelodeon and Disney were just getting off the ground.

Today, Nick and Disney are the major games in town with lots of original programming featuring young talent. At the same time, we can count on one hand the number of children who are series regulars on major network shows.

"There are not a lot of [network] shows with big roles for kids anymore," says veteran agent Judy Savage. "*Two and a Half Men* is just about the only one. Back in the eighties, there were twenty to thirty shows with young people in them. The last five years, there have been very few [network] pilots with kids. But it is changing again, and we're seeing more network pilots with kids this year. Also, kids are starring in films and making a lot more money than before."

One thing is for sure: For the past decade, kids have dominated cable TV. This shift seems logical, as a larger dial can support not only programs aimed at young people but also entire networks geared toward them. "There's been a boom in recent years," says Melissa Berger, a talent agent with CESD. "Big business has recognized how much money is to be made there with kids and tweens, and there are lots more projects out there that are geared toward the young talent."

But manager Bryan Leder of Bryan Leder Talent sums it up best: "As long as there are families on TV and in the movies, there will continue to be jobs in the youth market."

■ ■ ■

Now you've got a firm grasp on today's youth market. But before you run off to search for your big break, you need to prepare right here at home. The next chapter will help you get ready for your journey.

BEFORE YOU BEGIN,
START WHERE YOU BEGAN

Ian Nelson was fifteen years old and living in St. Paul, Minnesota, when a big Hollywood movie came to town. He headed over to the set to check out what all of the buzz was about and the lights, cameras, and action instantly mesmerized him. He started asking questions and soon found himself hired as an *extra* on the movie *Here on Earth*.

Ian's luck continued. The *director* liked his look and upgraded him to a bit part. Instead of working on the film for a few days, he was kept around for a few weeks. He even had a scene with the film's star, Leelee Sobieski. From this experience, Ian knew he wanted to be an actor and go to Hollywood one day.

"I wanted to get into the business locally and build my resume as much as I could," says Nelson.

But Ian wasn't impulsive. He finished school, signed up with a local talent agency, and did whatever jobs he could in the Minnesota area to gain experience and build his resume. When Ian felt he had accomplished everything he could in his hometown, he decided it was time to make the move to Los Angeles. His local agency used their Hollywood contacts to place him with representation on the West Coast.

"The plan was to move to L.A. and stay afloat as long as I could," says Nelson. "I knew I wanted to be in L.A., and nothing was stopping me."

In Hollywood, Ian was a small fish in a great big sea, but he loved getting his fins wet. He enrolled in a serious acting class and made great impressions on all of his auditions. Eventually, he started *booking* jobs: A national commercial for Burger King and a guest star role on an Aaron Spelling pilot were among his early successes.

After a few years, Ian had built an impressive resume. He was cast as a supporting lead in the film *Heavens Fall*. The first day on set, he met his fellow cast mates. The film's leading lady approached him and told him that he looked very familiar. Ian smiled and told her that the last time they had worked together, he had been an extra hired locally in Minnesota. Leelee Sobieski was quite impressed with how far her costar had come.

Home Sweet Home

One of the most common mistakes actors make is rushing out to Hollywood before fully preparing for their career right there at home. Believe it or not, there's a plethora of things you can do to get ready for a show business career without ever leaving your hometown. This chapter will outline many local opportunities that will help prepare you for your eventual move to a bigger market. We'll also help you determine when the time is right to make this move and which major market is best for your career.

The first thing you need to do is identify the mini-major market closest to you. You might live right in the heart of a major production center and not even realize it. Or, your nearest market might be a couple hours away. In any case, most major cities have some sort of media market, so find the one that's closest to you.

SOME OF THE BIGGER MINI-MAJOR MARKETS

Atlanta, Georgia

Boston, Massachusetts

Chicago, Illinois

Dallas, Texas

London, England

Miami, Florida

Montreal, Quebec

New Orleans, Louisiana

San Francisco, California

Sydney, Australia

Toronto, Ontario

Vancouver, British Columbia

Wilmington, North Carolina

Once you determine your local market, then you can create a game plan for maximizing the opportunities that market has to offer. If your closest market already happens to be Los Angeles or New York, then you've got a slight advantage. These are the two markets where all actors will eventually want to be.

School Ties

Many kids catch the show biz bug at school. They get involved with school plays, the music department, the AV club, or drama class, and they discover they have a talent or interest in performance. This type of experience is great when you are starting to build a resume. If you have professional ambitions, take advantage of every opportunity your school has to offer.

I always think it's a bit strange when I meet a kid who wants to be an actor, but he or she has never even participated in a school play. Don't let this be you. Being in a school play allows you to gain valuable experience and will help determine if acting is even the right career choice for you. If you don't get the lead role, don't get discouraged. Everybody has to start somewhere.

This advice isn't strictly for high school students, either. College students should also get involved as much as they can. And at most universities, you don't have to be a theater major to participate in a school production.

Many colleges also have film programs. At every film school, student filmmakers are constantly producing short films. Audition to be in as many student films as possible. You'll gain valuable experience while getting tape of yourself that could be used to build a *reel* down the road.

Basic Training

Some high schools offer acting, vocal, and/or dance training. But unless you attend a performing arts magnet, this training is probably very basic. However, basic training is the best way to start, if you haven't had any training at all. After a while, if you fail to be challenged by what you are learning in acting class, you probably need something more intensive.

There are a multitude of acting schools throughout the nation. Some of the more well known include the Academy of Cinema and TV (ACT), Barbizon Modeling, and John Robert Powers (JRP). Each school is owned and operated independently, so the quality of classes at one may not be the same as others. It's best to read reviews and do your homework on each individual program before signing up. Each program has its own procedures for admission, but typically it's a three-part process. The first part consists of a seminar where you are educated about the entertainment industry and the program being offered. Next comes an audition. The schools know that you probably have very limited experience, if any at all, so they're not expecting you to blow them away—it's more about seeing your personality shine in front of a camera. The final part usually involves an interview with you and your family, or just with you if you're an adult.

After this process is completed, you will find out if you have been selected to enter the program. If you get accepted, be sure that it's something you want to do because these schools are not inexpensive. However, the opportunity to learn and exercise your craft can be invaluable.

ACTING CLASSES

The Academy of Cinema and TV (ACT)
www.academyofcinemaandtv.com

Barbizon Modeling
www.barbizonmodeling.com

John Robert Powers (JRP)
www.johnrobertpowers.net

There are also hundreds of independent schools throughout the nation. Some of the ones at which I've found great talent include Honolulu's World Talent (www.worldtalentinc.com), Cleveland's Stone Models (www.stonemodels.com), and Cincinnati's Wings Model Management (www.wingsmodels.com). Check online to find independent schools in your area.

If you happen to live close to a major university with a decent theater program, you may be able to find a private coach in one of the professors there. Likewise, if you live close to a mini-major market, investigate casting directors and other members of the local film industry for coaching and classes. Be sure to explore all of these options.

Life Is a Stage

Maybe you're not in school, or, heaven forbid, your school district cut its funding for arts programs. There are still opportunities to get on stage with local *community theater*. In addition, there are great *regional theaters* throughout the heartland. While many of the lead roles in these productions are cast out of New York, the smaller roles often will be cast locally.

"Regional theater is the best place to hone your stagecraft without having to move to New York or Chicago," says Bryan Leder, a manager who represents a lot of successful stage actors. "You have a better chance of building your resume with quality roles that would typically go to names in a bigger market."

Many of the regional theaters bring in guest directors and choreographers. That makes it the perfect place to build relationships with these professionals. You also never know who might be watching in the audience on any given night.

"I was up in the Seattle area seeing a fantastic production of *Tommy* that one of my clients was starring in when a great performer in the ensemble caught my eye," recalls Leder. "Fast-forward a week. I had her in New York auditioning in front of the entire creative team for the Broadway production of *Spring Awakening*."

COMMUNITY AND REGIONAL THEATER RESOURCES

The American Association of Community Theater
www.aact.org

SELECTED REGIONAL THEATERS

Denver Center Theatre Company, Denver, Colorado
www.denvercenter.org

Gateway Playhouse, Bellport, New York
www.gatewayplayhouse.com

Lyric Theater, Oklahoma City, Oklahoma
www.lyrictheatreokc.com

North Shore Music Circus, Beverly, Massachusetts
www.nsmt.org

Continued on next page

Papermill Playhouse, Millburn, New Jersey
www.papermill.org

Pittsburgh Civic Light Opera, Pittsburgh, Pennsylvania
www.pittsburghclo.org

Stages, St. Louis, Missouri
www.stagesstlouis.com

Theater of the Stars, Atlanta, Georgia
www.theaterofthestars.com

Theater Under the Stars, Houston, Texas
www.tuts.com

Village Theatre, Issaquah and Everett, Washington
www.villagetheatre.org

ADDITIONAL REGIONAL THEATER LINKS
www.dl.ket.org/humanities/connections/theater/theatres.htm

America's Funniest Home Videos

The last book I wrote was called *15 Minutes of Fame: Becoming a Star in the YouTube Revolution.* In this book, I explored how to use sites like YouTube to launch your show business career. I interviewed many aspiring performers who made videos of their special talents, posted them to sites like YouTube, and then got discovered. I met a variety of artists, from aspiring musicians who posted original songs and got signed to record labels, to actors who uploaded comedy sketches and were subsequently signed to network development deals. What these artists all had in common was a great persona, an original concept, and a unique point of view.

The great thing about making your own videos and sharing them online is that you can do it from anywhere, no matter how geographically desirable to the industry you may or may not be. You'll not only gain experience, but you'll also be able to get immediate feedback on your work from other users. With any luck, these critiques will be constructive and will help you to learn and grow as an actor.

And who knows what talent scout might be watching? You just might get an e-mail from Hollywood out of the blue, as many performers have been able to launch their careers after being discovered online. Of course, for this to happen, you'll have to come up with something different that will draw enough attention to your videos, generate buzz, and catch the attention of industry professionals.

Maybe you're not ready to share your work with the World Wide Web. That doesn't mean you can't practice making short films on your video camera with friends. The more films you shoot, the better you will get. Having the chance to ham it up in front of the camera will help make you more comfortable when you ultimately land in the audition room and on professional sets.

Film Commission

The *film commission* is a government-run office in each state and most major cities that is responsible for anything having to do with local production. It can be a major resource to anyone wanting to break into the business on a local level.

The film commission can tell you what projects are going to be filming locally, who will be hiring extras, and who will be doing local casting for smaller roles. This office may also be able to refer you to neighborhood acting classes, regional agencies, and other nearby opportunities to get involved with the local filmmaking community. You can try calling your local film office, but many of them also have great websites with all sorts of resources and information available online.

Remember, on a show shot in Texas, for example, even though most major roles may be cast out of L.A., it would cost studios too much in travel and housing expenses to accommodate actors playing all of the smaller parts. A production will usually try to cast non-principals locally to keep costs down. Sometimes they'll even cast a larger role locally for that very same reason. While I've had clients lose out on a job or two to a local actor, I've also discovered a few talented local actors when they've made a great impression on TV.

Colin Fickes grew up in Raleigh, North Carolina. As a young boy he was bitten by the acting bug and signed up with a local talent agency. After being cast in a recurring role on *Dawson's Creek* (which happened to be shot about two hours from his hometown, in Wilmington), he packed his bags and headed to the Big Apple, where his resume stood out due to his professional credits.

With a few more roles under his belt, Fickes moved again, this time to Los Angeles, where he proceeded to get cast in another recurring role—on *One Tree Hill*. Ironically, like *Dawson's Creek*, this show also filmed in Wilmington. But instead of working as a local, he was hired out of Los Angeles.

Fickes says that a major difference of being cast locally is that usually the local casting director tapes the actor's audition and sends it off to the powers that be in Los Angeles, where the actors are literally cast off of the tape. "That tape is sent to producers and studio execs in L.A. or New York rather than them seeing you in person in the audition room."

The whole reason projects tend to cast locally is so that the studios can save money. But Fickes is quick to point out, "There are so many incredibly talented actors outside of L.A. and New York, and they are proving to Hollywood that not only can you cast extras locally but leading talent as well."

Casting local actors also benefits the project if the story actually takes place in the areas you are filming (as opposed to trying to substitute the locale for somewhere else). "It's often easier to get into character, having lived there and having a sense of the place," reveals Fickes. "Sense of place is so important in developing character, and knowing it well makes it easier to 'get there' as an actor.

"Having grown up in North Carolina where there have been so many opportunities to work as an actor, I've been so blessed," admits Fickes. "I was able to work on my craft, learn by being on set, and build up my resume so that I could be better prepared for New York and Los Angeles."

Although most projects are put together in Los Angeles, they are filmed all over the country, and all over the world. In fact, many major TV shows are filmed outside of L.A. and New York, including *Smallville* (Toronto), *Kyle XY* (Vancouver), *Prison Break* (previously Chicago, then Dallas), and *Friday Night Lights* (Austin, Texas), to name a few. These series generally cast locally for all of the smaller roles, including the classmates, wait staff, police force, inmates, football players, etc.

L.A., New York, and Everywhere in Between

Now that you've done everything you possibly can do locally and you're pretty sure you're ready to take that next step, the first decision you need to make is whether to go to Los Angeles or New York.

As a first consideration, where are you closer to geographically? If you live in New Jersey, Connecticut, or Philadelphia, for instance, you may want to focus on New York. If you live in San Diego, Santa Barbara, or Bakersfield, you should probably focus on Los Angeles. In each case, you will be close enough to these major cities to commute back and forth for auditions and meetings. Before you pick up and move your whole family, test the waters.

A second consideration may be where you have friends and family. If you already know someone in one of these two cities, perhaps they'll let you stay with them while you're getting situated. This can help you save money. Also, if you already have a network of friends and family in place, it makes moving to one of these big cities less overwhelming because you've already got a support system built in.

Quality of life is another important issue to think about. Do you want the sun and the sand of Los Angeles or the snow and humidity of New York? Do you want to be able to rely on public transportation in the Big Apple, or would you prefer to spend most of your days on the L.A. freeway system? While slightly exaggerated, these are real issues that you need to consider.

And of course, there is focus. Traditionally, Los Angeles is the mecca for everything related to film and television. However, TV production has been steadily growing in New York. If your focus is stage and musical theater, then New York is absolutely the place you want to be.

If your focus is on modeling or music, L.A. and New York aren't the only major markets. Miami, Milan, Tokyo, and Paris, for example, are great places to be if you're looking to succeed in the world of fashion. Singers and musicians often head for Orlando and Nashville. Regardless of the discipline or city, apply the same criteria we just discussed when making your decision about where to move.

Making the Move

If possible, try and have your representation ironed out before you make the big move. If you've got interest from a few companies, I always suggest taking an exploratory trip to meet with each person at their home base, before you make a final decision. If you don't have representation in place, that's okay. But getting an agent and a manager will have to be your primary focus once you set yourself up.

And you do need to get set up for success. You're probably so excited that you're finally in Hollywood and you want to jump right in! However, if you don't set yourself up properly, you'll only stumble. This happens more often with young adults who are on their own for the very first time navigating the city and life itself. But families moving here with younger children can easily fall into the same traps, so heed this advice:

Find a place to live. All the auditions in the world are not going to matter if you're too worried about where you're going to sleep at night. If you've got a friend who will let you crash on his or her couch, that's great—but remember, it's temporary. Be a good friend and make finding your own home a top priority.

Most rentals will require you to sign a one-year lease. However, if you're just coming out to test the waters, a few month-to-month options are available. Most come furnished, but these corporate housing options tend to be pricier. To save money, try a sublet. I've always found that Craigslist has a plethora of sublet listings in both L.A. and New York.

SHORT-TERM HOUSING OPTIONS

Oakwood Apartments: www.oakwood.com

Archstone Apartments: www.archstoneapartments.com

Craigslist: www.craigslist.com

Young adults should get a job that enables you to work at night, pays enough money to pay your bills, and is expendable.

You need to work at night so your days will be free for auditions. Most auditions occur between 10 A.M. and 6 P.M. Waiting tables, working at a gym, or staffing a hotel are all jobs that can be done at night.

You need to make enough money to pay your bills, but remember, you don't have to live like a movie star right now— that will come later. For now, cut costs as much as you can. Get a roommate. Don't buy the new flat-screen TV. And stop eating out every night!

Finally, you want the job to be expendable so you can quit it when you land your next acting gig. After all, you didn't move all the way from home to be a waiter for life. And you certainly didn't leave your family and friends behind so you could work full-time in an office to pay your rent.

If you move to Los Angeles, you *must* have a car. I'd even go so far as to suggest you have a navigation system (GPS) to make finding casting offices easier. After all, you don't want to be stressed about finding the place when you should be focused on getting into character and giving a great read. Of course if you can't afford a navigation system yet, just be sure to print out driving directions from Google Maps before you leave your apartment.

If you move to New York, *do not* bring a car. You'll spend all of your time, energy, and money on parking! The subway system in New York City is one of the best in the country. Get yourself a great subway map, and a MetroCard, and you'll be good to go.

■ ■ ■

Once you're all set up, you're ready for success. The next chapter will tell you whom you need to meet. Now rev up your engine, or hop on the train, and get ready to meet the players.

THE PLAYERS

Now that you're ready to advance your career to the next level, you need to put your representation in place. Having an effective team of handlers is essential to finding success in this industry. But before I discuss how to put a team together, I'll introduce the members of your starting lineup by explaining their roles as they relate to your career.

Think of your career as a business. Since it's your—or your child's—career, you (or they) are the chief executive officer of this new venture. In other words, you and/or your child are the final authority when it comes to career decisions.

Like the head of any company, you cannot make decisions in a vacuum. Instead, you want to surround yourself with the most knowledgeable advisors possible. That way, you can weigh all of your options, review the pros and cons of each opportunity, and then make the most educated choice you can.

Managers and Agents

Having a strong set of advisors whom you feel comfortable with and trust to guide your career is extremely important. The questions I am most often asked about agents and managers are: What is the difference? What do they do? How do you get one? How do you find the right one? This section will answer these questions and tell you everything you need to know about building the right team.

MANAGERS

If you are the CEO, then your manager is like the chief operating officer. Managers help their clients build the best business possible. In fact, managers would like to turn your start-up into a Fortune 500 company. One of their first responsibilities is to help you put together a team that will make your company flourish. This team will consist of various agents and other handlers, which I'll discuss below.

A manager's primary job is to guide and advise you on career matters. It is not to make decisions for you. An effective manager will present you with each opportunity and then discuss its positive and negative aspects to help you make the wisest choices for your career.

"I give my clients information to help them make the best decisions," says Bryan Leder. "But the client makes the ultimate decision—not me. I'll give my advice and let my opinion be known, but the client has the final say."

Some actors subscribe to the belief that when you're starting out, you don't have a career to manage, so why sign with a manager? Others recognize how competitive this business can be—especially in the youth market—and they want to build the strongest team possible, so they sign with a manager from the get-go.

"A newbie needs a manager for many important career-establishing reasons, such as to build credits and get exposure," suggests talent manager Susan Osser of Susan Osser Talent. "Building credits will help open doors as well as build a reel and resume. As this happens, the manager will communicate the progress and achievements to the agent. This is an important marketing process that continues as the actor grows.

"Managers keep in close communication with their client, agents, acting teacher, and/or private coaches," adds Osser. "This gives the actor the necessary guidance to stay on top of their game. A manager will make sure that *headshots* and pictures on industry sites are current and useful. A manager is the team leader, always watching out for opportunity, always building and promoting the actor in the direction of success."

As a manager I'm always looking at the big picture. How do I help launch a new client who has no resume at all? How do we move an actor from *costar* roles to "guest star only"? How do we build a reel to show casting directors and producers that a performer is ready to be a series regular? How do we make the transition from TV to film? How do we capitalize on the brand we've created by branching out into untapped areas like a clothing line or music career?

Managers tend to have a close personal relationship with their clients. This is mainly because management companies tend to be smaller than agencies, so a manager actually has the ability to talk to each client on a regular basis.

"I talk to some of my clients every day," reveals Leder. "Not everyone requires that type of hand holding, but for those who do, I make myself available. There's no such thing as a silly question, if getting it answered puts the client at ease."

Managers also make sure their clients are prepared for auditions and meetings. They follow up with casting directors to get feedback and share any constructive criticism with their actors. They make sure their talent are dressed appropriately, have updated resumes, consistently look like their headshots, and know where they're going. In essence, they handle the business side of your acting career, which leaves you free to focus on the craft and to nail each audition.

Of course, not all managers are the same. Not all clients are the same, either. Some actors need a lot more personal time and attention. Others are much more independent. I tend to find that as my clients' careers evolve, my role as manager also shifts to accommodate their changing needs. An actor who is just starting out has different needs, for example, than a client with her own series.

Managers do not get paid up-front and they do not make money until you start making money. Ever wonder how committed a manager is to your career? Look at how hard he or she has worked for you, especially at the beginning of your career, when you're not making much money at all. A good manager is happy to invest the time and energy into a client he or she believes in, no matter what stage of the acting journey you may find yourself on.

Most managers take a commission that is between 10 and 15 percent of your gross income for all jobs that you book. Music managers typically charge 20 percent. Managers should not commission income like *per diem* (spending money) or travel allowances.

When you're beginning your career, you want to find a management firm that has a solid reputation for developing new talent. The bigger companies like Brillstein Grey and The Firm really don't develop talent. They represent stars. But there are tons of smaller firms, like my own firm, Management 101, that have had many success stories breaking emerging talent. Some of these firms include Bryan Leder Talent, MC Talent, and Hines & Hunt.

There are so many management firms out there, that to list them all would fill volumes. However, I have included a select list in the appendix. Do your homework. Research each manager you meet. Type their names into Google. Find out what careers they've launched. And most important, make sure there's a personal connection and that they're on the same page about your career.

"When choosing a manager, look for someone who really has the best interest of your career at hand," says BLT's Bryan Leder. "You also want a manager who has strong relationships and experience that they can share with you. Many people look at the names that managers have on their list to determine their value. When starting out, you should research who got those names to where they are today."

"When looking for a manager, an actor needs to focus on many important qualities," adds Osser. "The manager should be well established in the industry with good credits. The manager should have several agents and agencies that they work with so that the actor can be put in an agency that is best for him or her. A newbie should look for a manager who does not have so many clients that the actor will not get the hands-on time they need to assist and guide them in the right direction. It is also important to pick a manager who is available when the actor calls and for there to be comfortable communication between actor and manager."

AGENTS

Talent *agents* are like employment agents: It's their job to get you a job. Unlike managers, agents are required to procure a license to do business. As such, their business practices are monitored by the government.

Like many businesses, your acting "business" may have multiple divisions, such as theater, commercial, voice-over, and print. You may decide to work with one agency that will cover you across the board and supervise all the divisions of your company. Or you may choose to team with different agencies that handle each division separately. In this case, one agent may handle you theatrically—for film and television— while another agent may handle you commercially for on-camera commercials. There may be an agency that handles your voice-over career for animation and radio ads. Still another agency might cover you for print and modeling work. Depending on your personal interests and goals, you may even have additional agents for your music or literary (writing and directing) career.

Each approach bears its own pros and cons. At a single agency it's often easier to get other departments behind you when they see you excelling in a specific arena. "It's really useful because I also cover voice-over," says Melissa Berger, an agent who works across the board with CESD. "When a client starts working for voice-over, I know he or she's going to be successful theatrically because you have to be a very good actor as a child to book a voice-over job. It helps with my theatrical pitching." When you're represented by multiple agencies, each agency can put all of their focus and energy into one individual part of your career without having to split their resources across the board. Personally, I've seen it work successfully both ways.

In addition to procuring work, an agent's other major function is to negotiate deals. Depending on the complexity of a deal, an entertainment attorney may be brought in as well (see page 51). Standard deal points, however, such as fees, credit, and dressing room, are generally handled by the agent.

Many actors wonder, "Do I need to have both an agent and a manager? If I'm just starting out, is there even a career to manage?" While the answers to these questions reflect a personal decision, I can only offer this advice: In an extremely competitive and ever-changing business, it is best to have as many people on your side fighting for you as possible.

I work with agencies both big and small. And all of my clients have agency representation. Effective handlers work together as a strong team, making sure clients do not miss out on any opportunities they are right for.

"My agent relationships are based on trust, reliability, work ethic, and communication," reveals talent manager Bryan Leder. "They need to have the same passion for the client as I do. At the end of the day it's my job to ensure that everyone is delivering what they signed up for, including me."

Like managers, agents also work on a commission basis only. They do not receive any money up front. Most agencies get 10 percent of your gross income. However, print and music agencies typically commission 20 percent of your gross income. Where a manager typically commissions all jobs, an agent will only commission jobs in the area that he or she covers. For instance, a **commercial agent** will commission the spot you just booked for Rice Krispies, but your theatrical agent will not touch that money. Likewise, a theatrical agent will commission the episode of *iCarly* you just shot, but the commercial agent will not be entitled to anything from that booking. In both cases, however, in addition to commissioning your appropriate agent, the manager will also take a percentage.

Agencies come in all different shapes and sizes. Some are small boutique companies with a limited number of agents and clients. Other firms are extremely large with hundreds and hundreds of clients. Because of their volume, the larger firms tend to have greater resources and access to information than some of the smaller firms. However, at a smaller firm, there is less of a chance for conflicts among clients and more of an opportunity to have a closer, personal relationship with the people working for you. "For kids, smaller agencies mean smaller client lists. That means less competition within the agency," explains Vivian Hollander, founder of Hollander Talent Group, an agency that specializes in young children. "More exposure is what all child actors should want. Larger agencies have larger lists and possibly more conflicts within the agency."

Some agencies and management firms specialize in specific age groups. For instance, a number of companies work exclusively with children, others work only with adults, and still others work with clients of all ages. I've included a select list of agencies in the appendix.

Many high-profile agencies specialize in the youth market. Some of the more notable ones include Abrams Artists, AKA, CESD, Coast to Coast, Innovative Artists, KSR, Osbrink, and the Savage Agency. Other agencies may represent youth talent among their client lists but do not have a separate department for this.

If you have a child or teen in the business, make sure you choose a company that works with children and teenagers. If you're an adult who plays kids or teens, you too should probably be with a company that specializes in the youth market.

There are certain advantages to being with a youth department. Mainly, casting directors know whom to call when they have an order to fill. Despite popular belief, casting companies don't always put out **breakdowns**, or casting notices, for every role they cast. Sometimes, with kids, they'll just place a few calls to some of the top youth agencies and let them know what they need. In turn, those agencies will send over their top kids in each category. If you're not with one of those agencies, you might miss out.

"Youth agencies and youth agents are the specialists when dealing with children. This is something that is well known to casting directors, directors, and producers," says Hollander. "They often will come to youth agents for suggestions and input, particularly if working with children is new to them. Adult agents and agencies have a totally different perspective when dealing with child actors."

Recently, two of the biggest agencies in town, the William Morris Agency (now William Morris Endeavor Entertainment) and United Talent Agency, both launched their own youth departments. This was a highly unusual move considering these powerhouse firms mainly handle big movie and TV stars. But as young talent like Taylor Momsen and Taylor Lautner become big stars themselves, it makes sense that the top agencies would expand to accommodate this emerging market. And for young actors who are just breaking into the business, this is great news. There's never been a better time for young people in Hollywood.

HOW TO GET REPRESENTATION

How do you choose a great agent and manager? This is a major decision, like purchasing a home or choosing a college. Proceed with caution.

It's important to understand that agents and managers choose you as much as you choose them. Think of it as a mutual interviewing process. When it comes to kids in the business, I not only interview them, but, concurrently, I interview the parents to make sure they're individuals I want to work with as well!

Before an actor comes to my office for a meeting, I've previously given her a scene to prepare so that I can see her work. When she comes in, I have her do the scene. Right away, I know if she is prepared. I also deduce that how she comes prepared to read for me is exactly how she'll arrive prepared for any audition I send her on. If I like what she did, I will generally give her an adjustment to see how she handles direction.

The second part of our meeting will consist of an informal interview. It's a chance for me to get to know the actor and a chance for the actor to get to know me. I'll ask about things I see on her resume, and I'll inquire about her career goals. If I feel that this is an actor who could benefit from my services, I'll ultimately offer her representation.

The absolute best way to find representation is through referral. Someone you know sends your headshot to an agent or manager that he knows. A casting director or producer whom I respect sends me an actor's reel and suggests I take a meeting with him. One of my clients refers her friend who isn't a conflict and who she thinks is a great performer.

But what if you don't know anyone who can give you a referral? You want to be more proactive. Take advantage of living in Los Angeles and get yourself seen. You can accomplish this by performing in a showcase that representatives attend, doing local theater, and participating in acting seminars or workshops taught by industry professionals. You can find information on all of these opportunities in the trade publications listed in the appendix.

If you're not living in New York or Los Angeles, but you're trying to crack the major markets, post videos of your work online to sites like YouTube (see page 16). Successful videos often attract the attention of Hollywood. Another great way to get in front of agents and managers is to participate in a talent convention (see page 37). While this may not be an inexpensive way to meet industry professionals, it can be highly effective.

SCOUT'S HONOR

As a manager, one of my functions is that of talent scout. I'm constantly looking for fresh, untapped talent with abundant potential that I can develop and represent. Discovering and launching new careers is one of the most rewarding parts of my job. In fact, there's no better feeling than to tell a new client that she just booked her first acting gig.

Finding great talent isn't an easy feat. I never know where I'll find that next big star. As such, my scouting radar is constantly on. Whether I'm at the mall, on the beach, or on a movie set, the cogs in my brain are always churning. It's not that I'm actively looking for new clients. I just seem to be extremely aware of those around me—especially when they possess that all-important "It factor."

"The 'It factor' is that special sparkle that emanates from that very special talent," claims agent Vivian Hollander. "It is something that taps into the desires of young kids who attend movies and watch TV. Defining it is almost impossible. One just knows it when one sees it."

"The 'It factor' is that intangible quality you can't put your finger on—that magical spark," concurs casting director Lauren Bass. "It's an immediate reaction—you are either drawn to someone or you are not. From a casting perspective, it's all about intrigue. You think, is there something interesting about this person? Does this person have a story to tell?"

Periodically, I attend specific functions and events dedicated to scouting. For instance, I may watch a showcase one night with the sole purpose of looking at a group of actors perform scenes. I may spend a day at a small acting school outside of Los Angeles hoping for a great find. I'll attend talent conventions where I can see hundreds, if not thousands, of potential actors engaging in various competitions that showcase their skills.

CONVENTIONS

A lot of conventions get bad press. You research them online and find websites where attendees claim they were scammed. While I can't say that there hasn't ever been a talent competition that had unethical practices, for the most part these are legitimate businesses that provide a door into the industry.

At the conventions I have attended, aspiring actors attend seminars to learn about the business. They also have an opportunity to perform in competitions and vie for prizes while at the same time audition for industry professionals. Often, the conventions program networking mixers where actors can mingle with industry pros. And the events generally end with a *callback* session so that agents and managers can talk one-on-one with any actors they wish to pursue.

I believe in them because I have found some amazing clients through them. If I hadn't been at the now defunct Talent Rock, I never would have discovered Andrew Caldwell (see page 44). In fact, when I attend these conventions now, I always say if I can just find one Andrew every time, I'm golden.

But because not everyone gets a callback or books the job at conventions, people get upset. They've spent thousands of dollars to meet Hollywood agents and leave with nothing. Instead of becoming angry, they should look at their convention experiences as a wakeup call. Performers and parents should realize that perhaps they or their children just may not be competitive enough for the business right now. Or maybe acting just isn't what they're meant to do. Learn from this experience, get the training you need to excel, and then try again. I bet you'll see different results.

SELECTED CONVENTIONS

» **Name:** Actors, Models & Talent Competition
Website: www.AMTCworld.com
What makes it different: "AMTC is Christian based,"
says CEO Carey Arban. "Our first goal is to honor God.
Our second goal is to educate, uplift, and promote the
families that trust their hopes, dreams, and talent to us."
Success stories: Adair Tishler (*Heroes*), Mitch Holleman
(*Reba*), Allie Grant (*Weeds*)
Established: 1982

» **Name:** International Modeling and Talent Association
Website: www.imta.com
What makes it different: "IMTA is a one-of-a-kind event,"
says Nancy Mancuso, chief operating officer. "It is the
only week-long event that provides attendees the
exposure to so many agents, managers, casting direc-
tors, and industry professionals, as well as a number of
educational seminars offered and one-on-one interviews.
Those attending compete in age-appropriate divisions
that range from four years old to mature adults. There is
nothing like the IMTA experience!"
Success stories: Brandon Routh (*Superman Returns*),
Ashton Kutcher (*What Happens in Vegas*), Eva Longoria
(*Desperate Housewives*), Elijah Wood (*Lord of the Rings*),
Jessica Biel (*I Now Pronounce You Chuck and Larry*),
Katie Holmes (*Batman Begins*), Jerry Ferrara
(*Entourage*), Seann William Scott (*Role Models*), and
Sean Faris (*Never Back Down*), to name a few.
Established: 1987

» **Name:** International Presentation of Performers
Website: www.ipopconvention.com
What makes it different: "It's an event that happens twice a year: once in Las Vegas and once in Hollywood," says agent director Philip Leader, who is also a partner in Brown Leader Management Group. "It brings trained performers from JRP [John Robert Powers] schools who get to meet with agents and managers from all over the world. We also bring out kids from as far away as Canada and London. But it's not just for JRP students. We also do road shows throughout the United States and conduct training for these kids before the actual event happens."
Success stories: Devon Conti (*The Changeling*), Doug Brochu (*Sonny with a Chance*), Billy Unger (*The Last Medallion: The Adventures of Billy Stone*), and Cole Cockburn (*Tree of Life*).
Established: 2005

» **Name:** Model & Talent Expo
Website: www.modelandtalentexpo.com
What makes it different: "I always try to keep it below four hundred attendees, because I want these kids to have time in front of the agents," explains Expo president Mike Beaty. "We keep the agent ratio to one agent for every ten kids. We've found amazing people who would have been lost if they had been at one of those big conventions."
Success stories: Country singer Miranda Lambert, Chase Coleman (*One Life to Live*), and Justin Gaston (*Nashville Star*).
Established: 1992

Continued on next page

» **Name:** Model & Talent Search Canada
Website: www.mtsc.ca
What makes it different: "We are the largest and the most affordable in Canada," says Kate Godard, director of agent relations. "Attendees do not require training/schooling and/or extensive/expensive pictures. We hold several events in major cities across Canada, bringing the agents to the potential models/actors rather than having them have to incur the expense of traveling to see the agents. We are the only organization that limits attendance, therefore we boast the highest 'agent to contestant' ratio. We have open go-sees for everyone, not just callbacks."
Success stories: Chrislyn Austin (*Two for the Money*), Katie Todd (*Radio Free Roscoe*), and Brandon Olds (*The Sandlot 3*)
Established: 1994

» **Name:** The (pronounced "Tay")
Website: www.expthe.tv
What makes it different: According to Nathan Biay, director of The, "Ours is smaller that the others, so there's more opportunity to stand out."
Success stories: This is the newest event on the circuit, so check their website to see what success stories emerge.
Established: 2008

WHAT ARE YOU LOOKING FOR?

People always ask me what I'm looking for when scouting talent. The truth is, I don't know what I'm looking for, but I know it when I see it. I equate discovering talent with falling in love for the first time. If you go out to a bar looking for love, you're probably not going to find it. However, when you meet the right guy or girl, you'll just know it. The same holds true for talent.

That said, there are four general parameters that I do look for. If I'm going to sign someone, chances are they excel in all of the following areas.

You've Got the Look Don't worry. You don't need to look like Joe Jonas or Ashley Tisdale. But if you do, that'd be okay, too. In fact, if you've ever watched TV or seen a movie before (and let's be real . . . who hasn't?), you've probably noticed that there are all sorts of different types on screen. That means all ethnicities, all shapes, all sizes, and actors of every form possible. In fact, diversity is essential to programming today.

When I produced *Dance on Sunset*, the other producers and I knew we wanted to have a diverse cast. However, we didn't set out to cast "the Caucasian one, the African-American one, the Latin one, etc." But we luckily found a great cast of talented kids who just happened to be multiethnic.

While most talent representatives are open to any and all looks, there is one look we tend *not* to go after: anyone who looks like a client we already represent. That wouldn't be fair to you, and it wouldn't be fair to our client. Barring that, we're pretty much open to anyone.

You Light Up My Room If you are introverted and shy, then this might not be the right business for you. You've got to have an amazing personality to succeed. For better or worse, personality is not something you can create—it's something you're born with. You have to be real when you walk in a room—if you're pretending to be someone you're not, we can see right through it. So just relax, be yourself, and show us your natural energy and charm. You'll win us over with your charisma and enthusiasm as you light up the room.

Raise Your Hand if You're Sure I truly believe the difference between booking a job and not booking a job is confidence. When you walk in a meeting, you need to own the room. But what do I mean by that?

You need to walk into an audition as if you've already booked the job. You've arrived on set, the lights are on, and the director yells, "Action!" If you've done your homework and are completely prepared, you should be able to nail it.

Remember, it's not about ego or cockiness. Don't go in with a big head, but be sure of yourself. After all, you are prepared. You know your stuff. You have just as good a chance as anyone to book this role. Your confidence in the room will transfer to the decision makers and they will feel comfortable casting you in the part. That said, you can have all the confidence in the world, but sometimes nerves just get in the way. I find that the more times you put yourself into a public speaking or audition situation, the easier it gets. Eventually your nerves will relax and confidence will become second nature. For more on auditioning, see chapter 6.

Last but Not Least The last thing I look for, and perhaps the most obvious . . . is talent. You must have some degree of talent if you want me to consider representing you. That doesn't mean I expect Abigail Breslin or the Sprouse Brothers to walk into the room . . . although it would be great if they did. But I need to see some potential talent inside of you when you read for me.

With the right coaching and development, you can get to a competitive level—where you'll be able to book jobs against the best of them. But know that to do that, it may take a lot of hard work. After all, acting is a muscle. And like any muscle, you need to work out frequently to stay strong and toned. If you work out in a gym once a week, or once a month, or not at all, you probably won't have a very defined body. But if you work out every day, or several times a week, you'll have a pretty solid physique.

Acting is the same way. If you never go to class, or work on a script, or practice your craft . . . then when that big audition comes along, and you realize several weeks, or several months, have gone by since you last picked up a script, you probably won't make a very good impression in the audition room. However, if you've been practicing and working out your acting muscle on a regular basis, then when that big audition comes along, you will more than likely be prepared. You'll go in and leave a positive lasting impression. It's this acting muscle, and all of its potential, that I'm scouting for.

NOT ANOTHER TEEN STAR

Andrew Caldwell has appeared in dozens of TV shows and films. You may know him best as Thor from Disney Channel's *Hannah Montana* or as Bubba Bixby in Nickelodeon's original movie *Shredderman Rules!* Others may know him from his roles in *Transformers* or *College*. I still remember the very first time I met Andrew.

He was fourteen years old. He had bleached blond hair and braces. He stood at about five feet six inches and weighed about 220 pounds. He sure didn't look like a star.

But when he walked into my audition room (I found him at a talent convention), the minute he opened his mouth, the whole energy of the room changed. I had just seen a group of forty boys mutilate the same commercial copy again and again. But Andrew brought so much charisma and confidence to the work that everybody just gravitated to his energy. Within seconds, I knew he would be a star and I knew that I wanted to work with him.

BLIND SUBMISSIONS

When all else fails, there's always the blind submission. Despite what some people may think, I look at every submission that comes across my desk. That doesn't mean I call in everyone to read for me, but occasionally there's someone whose headshot or resume catches my eye.

When Carla Renata sent me her headshot and resume, I was immediately impressed. First, here was an actor who wasn't a conflict with any of my other clients. Second, her resume caught my attention with costar credits on many top

TV shows, from *Frasier* to *Will & Grace*. But the kicker was that she noted a connection to me in her cover letter. She wrote that she had heard me speak at a seminar I gave at UCLA, and she was impressed with what I had to say. Okay, so she stroked my ego. Who doesn't like that? I quickly set up a meeting.

What happened in the meeting would determine whether I would offer her representation. Her engaging personality brightened my day. I laid out a game plan as to what I would do to help advance her career. She liked my ideas and told me we were on the same page. I didn't need her to read for me because she showed me an amazing reel. I offered her representation on the spot.

Since signing Carla, we've achieved so many of the things we set out to do. She stopped doing costar roles and started doing guest star appearances only on such shows as *CSI*, *Reba*, and *The Suite Life of Zack & Cody*. She tested for a series regular role on a pilot, which she had never done before. And she went back to Broadway in a lead role (another first) in the Tony Award–winning show *Avenue Q*. I continue to look through every blind submission I receive because you never know when the next Carla might be in the mail.

The Rest of Your Team

In addition to an agent and manager, there are others you can add to your team. Some, like a strong acting coach, you'll want to choose right away. Others, like a ***publicist*** or entertainment lawyer, you may not need until your career starts to progress. In any event, these people, and a few others, are introduced below.

ACTING COACH

An acting coach can be a valuable member of your team. Some actors take group classes. Others prefer to work one-on-one with a coach. Still others use a combination of both techniques. Having the right coach can sometimes give you the competitive edge that you need to book a job.

Tanya Berezin is one of the top acting coaches in the business. Her clients include Bobby Cannavale (*Cupid*), Jake Cherry (*A Night at the Museum*), and Brandon Routh (*Superman Returns*). Before his first audition for *Superman Returns*, Routh worked with Berezin. But when Routh found out he was going to move forward and screen-test to be the Man of Steel, his coach was back in New York. This was the role of a lifetime—and they both knew it—so Berezin hopped on a plane and came back to Los Angeles to work with her student.

Before the *test*, they worked together over a three-day period, for two to three hours a day. The first day, all Berezin did was ask Brandon questions about the character. *Who is this guy? What was he made of?* She wanted Routh's answers to be as specific as possible. The next two days they just worked on the scenes.

Berezin believes that the real magic begins once the actor walks away from the coaching session and the work they've done filters into his or her DNA. "When you sleep on it—that is when the work becomes the actor's, rather than the coach as director," she reveals.

How was Berezin able to help Routh withstand the intense pressure and hype that landing this career-changing role would create? "You need to work on each scene as if you've already booked the job and you start shooting tomorrow—*not* as if you are being judged," says Berezin. The advice took. Routh booked the job and went from struggling actor to movie star overnight.

Private coaching is not cheap: Prices can run anywhere from $50 to $200 an hour. During busy times—like pilot season, for instance—coaches' schedules book up fast. So the moment you know of an important audition, the next call you make should be to your coach to set up a private session.

Choosing the right coach and acting class are crucial tasks. Not every coach or acting teacher is right for every actor. You want to find a place where you feel comfortable to express yourself and open up. But you also want to find someone who challenges you and makes you work hard so that you continue to grow as an actor. I recommend meeting one-on-one with a coach to discuss your goals before hiring him or her for a private session. I also highly recommend auditing an acting class before you jump in and register, to see if it's right for you.

ACTING COACHES AND CLASSES

There are so many acting classes to choose from, I couldn't possibly list them all. But the list below includes classes that my own clients have had good results with over the years.

SCENE STUDY

Janet Alhanti: www.janetalhantistudios.com

Deke Anderson: www.nextlevelacting.com

Cynthia Bain: www.cynthiabain.com

Joanne Baron: www.baronbrown.com

Martin Barter: www.themeisnercenter.com

Continued on next page

Vicki Baumann: www.vickibaumann.com
Tanya Berezin: www.tanyaberezin.com
Bobbie Chance: www.bobbiechance.com
Ivana Chubbuck: www.ivanachubbuck.com
Howard Fine: www.howardfine.com
Diane Hardin: www.dianehardinacting.com
Lesly Kahn: www.leslykahn.com
Milton Katselas: www.bhplayhouse.com
Kristopher Kyer: www.kyerworkshop.com
Dennis Lavalle: www.lavalleactorsworkshop.com
David Legrant: www.studioforacting.com
Marlene Mancini: www.hbstudio.org
Michelle Manner: www.edgemarcenter.org
Eric Morris: www.ericmorris.com
Larry Moss: www.larrymossstudio.com
Lane Napper: www.lanenapper.com
Playhouse West: www.playhousewest.net
John Sarno: www.johnsarnostudio.com
Scott Sedita: www.scottseditaacting.com
Aaron Speiser: www.aaronspeiser.com
Scott Tiler: www.scotttiler.com
Doug Warhit: www.dougwarhit.com
Michael Woolson: www.michaelwoolson.com

COLD READ

Margie Haber: www.margiehaber.com
Laura Henry: www.laurahenrystudio.com
John Homa: www.johnhoma.com
Joe Palese: www.theactorspace.com
Brian Reise: www.brianreiseacting.com
Cameron Thor: www.carterthorstudio.com

IMPROV AND COMEDY

Acme Comedy Theater: www.acmecomedy.com
Bill Applebaum: www.actorsimprovstudio.com
Judy Carter (stand up): www.judycarter.com
The Groundlings: www.groundlings.com
Improv Olympics: www.ioimprov.com
Harvey Lembeck:
www.harveylembeckcomedyworkshop.com
Paul Ryan: www.paulryanproductions.com
Second City: www.secondcity.com
Upright Citizen's Brigade: www.ucbtheatre.com

VOICE, SPEECH, AND DICTION

Act 4 Reel: www.act4reel.com
Sue Blu: www.blupka.com
Bob Corff: www.corffvoice.com
Robert Easton: www.roberteaston.org
Tony Gonzales: www.kidsvo.com

COMMERCIALS

Craig Colvin: www.cocolaca.com/classes.html
Lien Cowan Casting: www.leancow.tv
Stuart Robinson: www.stuartkrobinson.com

PUBLICIST

A publicist's job is to generate buzz and create publicity opportunities for a client. But publicists can be expensive. Make sure you have something to publicize if you're going to pay out $3,000 to $4,000 a month for these services. While most TV series and films hire their own publicists to promote their projects, some actors prefer to hire a personal publicist whose sole function is to help promote the actor.

"A few years ago, there was a kid who never worked, but he had a publicist," recalls agent Judy Savage. "We constantly got stuff [articles, publicity photos, etc.] from this kid—but it didn't create work for him. The time you need publicity is when you've already got work—it's to publicize the work you've already done. A publicist needs three to six months' lead time to do the job right."

"Publicity is very important to a young actor's career," says veteran Hollywood publicist Ron Scott. "The minute an actor is booked for a role in a film, TV series, or stage production, it's time to start the publicity.

"The main goal is to make the public aware of the actor and to start building a strong fan following," says Scott. "Just as important, the publicity campaign should create awareness of the actor among the members of the entertainment industry who hire them for future jobs. Casting directors, writers, producers, and directors pay attention to the buzz on a new artist."

When launching careers, publicists try to spread the word and create excitement about their clients. They set up interviews with various media outlets, including print, radio, television, and Internet. They also seek photo opportunities and often will get their clients on the list for hot clubs and movie premieres where they can get their pictures taken on the red carpet. In essence, they do whatever they can do to generate excitement about their clients.

But unless your name is Miley Cyrus or Zac Efron, publicity for kids can be a tricky nut to crack. It's still important, because any publicity—even a tiny mention in the smallest periodical—is helpful. But keep your expectations as realistic as possible. "I don't care how many publicists you've got trying to get you in there, the big shows (like *Good Morning America* or *Regis & Kelly*) want to talk to the stars," adds Savage. "They don't want to talk to the kids. Unless the kid is the absolute star of the picture and it's an absolute phenomenon, that's a different story. They're going to push these kids out of the way on the red carpet because right behind them is a star—and it might not even be a star from their film. I've been on the red carpet and watched it happen."

ENTERTAINMENT ATTORNEY

Whenever you're dealing with contracts and legalese, it is always a good idea to consult an attorney. A few hundred dollars up front could save you thousands later on. That said, when you're just starting out, you probably don't need the full-time services of an entertainment lawyer.

In general, the first time you might need legal assistance is when you sign a contract with representation. While most agent and manager contracts are fairly straightforward and standard, it's always a good idea to have them looked over by a professional prior to signing. You should also get in the habit of reading over contracts and understanding as much of the fine print as possible. Understand how you are paid, how much services cost, and where the money goes. A good attorney can help explain these details to you. As such, if you don't know an entertainment attorney, any general counsel can proofread a contract and offer his advice.

As your career evolves, an entertainment attorney can become an essential part of your team. Deals get more complicated, and some agents may not feel comfortable with the finer points of the multipage agreements. While the larger agencies have their own *business affairs* departments to navigate these deals, many actors bring their own lawyers to the table to advise and negotiate in these matters.

"I think it's important to meet with attorneys early on," says entertainment lawyer Hartford Brown with the law firm Klinedinst PC in Los Angeles. "However, you generally don't need one on board until contract negotiations begin or when that first contract hits the door, whichever is first."

Most entertainment attorneys work on a commission basis at a rate of 5 to 10 percent. However, some bill by the hour. And most bill hourly when it comes to anything other than contract work. So always ask about their rates and fees before enlisting their services.

BUSINESS MANAGER

Once you are earning significant money, you will need to retain the services of a good business manager. This financial professional can advise and assist in forming a corporation for protection and tax purposes and can also consult on financial planning. A business manager can let you know which career-related expenses you can write off, as well as how to handle your cash flow. As you would when searching for any other member of your team, be sure to do your homework and check references before hiring a business manager to handle the income you've worked hard to earn.

STUDIO TEACHER

When you're under eighteen and still in school, the state requires that you devote a certain number of hours each day you work to your education. Provided by each production, a *studio teacher* is someone whose function is to monitor the safety of any children on set and to help them with their educational requirements by tutoring them so they can keep up with their schoolwork while they are shooting.

Unlike the rest of your team, you don't always get to choose your studio teacher. Then again, you probably didn't get to pick your teachers in high school, either. Sometimes the teacher can be negotiated into a deal, but it's not always guaranteed.

Other People You Should Know

There are a few other people you need to know about to gain a better understanding of how the entertainment industry operates. While these people are not members of your personal team per se, their help and respect can assist you in making a successful career.

CASTING DIRECTORS

Casting directors are hired to find the best actor for each role in a project. Think of them as human resources reps for film, television, and stage productions. A group of about fifty casting directors cast 90 percent of all projects in Los Angeles. A group of about twelve casting directors cast 90 percent of all projects in New York.

Lauren Bass has cast a variety of film and television projects including the *feature* *Eloise in Paris* and the Nickelodeon series *Dance on Sunset*. "When meeting an actor for the first time, I look for a natural quality, an ease," she reveals. "I want someone who is comfortable with himself, someone who isn't trying to perform."

The first thing the Casting Company's Michelle Lewitt looks for is to see if, visually, an actor is right or believable in the role. "No matter how brilliant someone is at their craft, if you look twenty-five and I need an eighteen-year-old, there is no getting around that," says Lewitt.

Second, she considers the actor's preparation. "If an actor is prepared, it not only speaks to his professionalism, but it also lets me know how much I can direct him," says Lewitt. "It's almost impossible to effectively direct an actor who has his face stuck in the page because he doesn't have the material sufficiently prepared."

Lewitt, who was a casting director on such films as *Transformers*, *Jack and the Beanstalk*, and *I Love You Beth Cooper*, can't stress preparation enough. "From knowing the material and your character, to knowing the type of film or TV show it is, to knowing the filmmakers involved, it makes a difference," she reveals. "If you come in for a David Fincher movie and have prepared your scene like a Woody Allen movie, it's not going to go well."

The biggest misconception about casting directors is that they just want to say no and move on to the next audition. After all, they've got hundreds of actors to see in a very short amount of time. But this isn't the case at all. In fact, a casting director is an actor's greatest ally. They want desperately for each and every performer to be "the one." After all, as soon as they cast a role, they can move on to the next one!

There are all types of casting directors. Some work exclusively by medium (film, TV, theater, commercials, voice-over, etc.). Others work across the board. The best casting directors I've found will see the same potential that I see in a performer, and then they'll work with that actor to get the best performance out of her, so that when she goes to callbacks, she'll nail the audition.

PRODUCERS

Producers wear many hats. Some find the money to get a project made. Others create and develop the concept. Some are producers by virtue of the fact that they bring star talent to the table. Others physically supervise the production from beginning to end. One big job that producers perform is deciding who will ultimately get each role. Most callbacks are with producers. Callbacks are an opportunity for the casting director to show his boss (the producer) the top choices for each role.

I generally tell my clients that when a casting director brings you to meet the producers, he's basically telling the producers that any of his top choices would be great for the job. It's now time for the producers to choose who they like best. Whatever the actor did in the room the first time should be repeated in the callback.

In television, the producers are also generally the writers, and they have the most creative power aside from the production company and network that finance and air the show, respectively. In film, it is the director who has the most creative power aside from the studio that is financing and distributing the film. In theater, you will meet with the entire creative team—which generally consists of the producers, the director, and, if appropriate, the musical director—at callbacks.

EVERYONE ELSE

There are a slew of other people with whom you will interact once you book a job. These include members of the crew, everyone in the director's unit, the hair, makeup, and costume team, production managers, and *craft services*. It's a very good idea to get to know who these people are and how they function on set. There are many great books available that explain each and every one of their roles. Please see the appendix for a list of books I recommend. I encourage you to get familiar with the rest of the crew positions so you have a leg up when you're working on set for the first time.

You—And How You Fit In

This point bears repeating, so I'm writing it again: YOU ARE THE DECISION MAKER. IT IS YOUR CAREER. Your team works for you. At the end of the day, you need to look to your team and heed their advice so that you can make smart decisions about your career.

When an actor gets his first agent, he's very excited that someone signed him. It may have felt intimidating going to the agency, reading for the agent, and essentially auditioning to be a client of the firm. But remember, as much as you are auditioning for representation, they, too, are auditioning for you.

As you meet people in your journey, it should be your objective to develop as many relationships as possible with industry professionals. They may not be able to help you now, but there might be some way for you to work together in the future.

When you're first meeting casting directors, you want to win them over so that they become fans. When you're meeting with representation, you want to leave a great impression.

That said, be careful how you treat people—especially those who work for you. Today's agent could be tomorrow's producer. If something went wrong with your relationship when you were an agent's client, you certainly wouldn't want that to have an impact on being able to work with him in the future. You could go back to him for representation, or you may discover that he has taken on a new role in the entertainment industry. Always act professionally and courteously. Sometimes things don't work out; it happens. But this is a really small business, and you just never know when you might work with someone again.

■ ■ ■

In the next chapter, I'll discuss the importance of having a great headshot and resume, as well as other effective selling tools. If you decide to do a mailing seeking representation, you may as well put your best foot forward.

THE TOOLS

Jenni Livingston thought she had seen it all: big hair, crazy outfits, kids who couldn't sit still. I consider her to be one of the best headshot photographers in the business. And I always recommend her to clients who are in need of new pictures.

One day a client brought in her proof sheet for me to see. She was over eighteen, but she looked very young. As I browsed the proofs of the photos Jenni had shot, immediately I realized she had way too much makeup on. In fact, she had so much on that the photos made her look older than she really was, and much older than she generally plays.

I called Jenni and asked her about the makeup. Usually she's good about telling the girls to use very light makeup for her shoots. She thought the actress had removed the makeup before they started shooting but volunteered to take a few more rolls since we couldn't use the pictures.

The photos from the second shoot came back and there was a big improvement over the first time. However, the client still appeared to have a great deal of eye makeup on. I called Jenni again to ask about this.

"Frederick, I thought I'd seen everything," Jenni started. "This girl has eye liner tattooed to her face."

How I had never noticed this before is beyond me. But I'll never in a million years understand why an actress would do that to her face. Let alone a woman who could still be playing fifteen-year-olds if she hadn't applied permanent makeup.

We never did get a great headshot. For a while we continued to use her old one, shot prior to her inking. Needless to say, she didn't remain a client of our firm for much longer after this incident.

Headshot

An actor's headshot is his business card. Your representation submits headshots to casting directors to help solicit auditions. It is generally your way of introduction to new representatives and casting directors. As such, it must make a great first impression. "I look for an honest moment captured," says manager Bryan Leder. "It shouldn't feel forced or posed. For me it's all about the eyes."

"A headshot has to resonate energy and personality from the child so that it immediately says 'this is a special child,'" says agent Vivian Hollander.

Because so many breakdowns instruct talent reps to submit photos online, it's always a good idea to bring a hard copy of your headshot to meetings to leave behind for the casting director. Headshots are eight inches wide and ten inches long. They can be vertical or horizontal, with or without borders, and with or without your name on the front. Everyone has their own opinions about what they want headshots to look like and how they prefer them printed. To even suggest a standard would be doing you a disservice, because the people you work with will want them done to their unique specifications. What I will share, however, is how I like them done—and this should at least get you started.

I like to see a traditional headshot that captures not much more than the performer's face. I prefer a horizontal shot to a vertical shot because the actor can fill the frame better when the shot is taken sideways. In a horizontal shot posted next to vertical shots on the same wall, the actor appears larger than life and draws more attention from onlookers.

No one uses black-and-white film anymore. You shouldn't, either. Everything is shot in color these days. I prefer outdoor, natural lighting to inside studio lights. I like little to no makeup on girls and no makeup whatsoever on boys. Actors should dress their age in casual, generic (no brands or logos visible), comfortable clothes.

Many actors have multiple headshots, but do not put more than one photo on an 8 × 10 page. Typically, I like my clients to have a theatrical shot—which features a more serious, neutral palette—with no strong facial expression. I also would want you to have a commercial headshot, which I would also use for lighter fare like half-hour sitcoms and comedy films. Generally, you would be smiling in this photo. Since almost all commercial submissions (in Los Angeles) are done online, I generally choose multiple commercial shots for each client. Since actors don't need to have them all reproduced, just scanned into a computer, having options isn't cost prohibitive like it may have been years ago. While the commercial industry in New York is using more electronic casting today than ever before, they still rely heavily on hard copy submissions. The breakdown should indicate whether casting directors prefer hard copy or electronic submissions.

Most likely, I would have you print your name on the front of your picture, just underneath the border. Again, whether that name is left or right justified is just a personal preference. Some agencies prefer all their clients to do it one way so that their submissions have a uniform look. One agency I work with prefers a full bleed, with no border, so that it forces the casting director to turn the picture over to see the actor's name and, in doing so, automatically spy the resume that's attached to the back of the photo on a hard-copy submission.

It doesn't matter to me if your pictures are printed on photo paper or lithographs. Because so much of the submission process is done electronically, actors go through much fewer photos than they used to. You still need to bring a copy of your headshot with you every time you go to an audition. If you are trying to cut costs, I'd recommend the litho prints.

When you get to the audition, you must look like your photo. One of the biggest mistakes actors make is that they touch up their photos so much that they don't look like them, or their pictures are so old that they look like them ten years ago. When casting calls you in based on your photo, you better believe they want to see the person in the photo walk in the room.

Michelle Lewitt of the Casting Company offers a casting perspective: "A headshot needs to actually look like the actor in front of me," she says. "I don't care if it's black and white or color or sepia, but if the person in the picture looks nothing like the person in front of me (with hair/facial hair being exceptions, because that changes all the time), it's a waste of everyone's time. You want to be brought in for roles you have a chance of getting, and having a truthful headshot helps make that happen."

Kids are always growing and changing, and as a result they need to update their photos constantly. This can get expensive, but it is a necessary evil. Mom and Dad, be prepared to do new photo shoots every year as your child gets older.

Resume

When you flip a headshot over, a resume should always be stapled to the back. Don't print the resume on the back of the photo, because hopefully it will need to be updated consistently and then the pictures will no longer be valid. Why waste perfectly good prints? Instead, print out a resume before each audition and staple it to the back of your headshot. Some agencies will prefer the resume to be cut to size to fit the 8 × 10 photo exactly. I don't care as long as it's stapled (face out) to the back of the headshot. Resumes need to fit on one page. No one is going to flip through a ten-page resume. And even the top actors in the world can fit their work experience on a single page. You should be able to as well.

Let's start with the basic information every resume should have on it. At the top, list your full name. You're not a superstar yet, so no need to drop the last name at this point in your career. Doing so will only make you look like a diva, and that is not what you want to portray at all.

Kids' resumes should include their vital statistics: height, weight, hair and eye color, and date of birth. If you are over eighteen but play younger, do not print your date of birth. Instead, simply list that you are legal eighteen. An audition is a job interview, and it's technically illegal for a casting director to ask your age. For my adult clients who no longer play under eighteen, I usually leave all the vitals and age off the resume completely.

This next one might seem obvious, but you'd be amazed at how many people don't do it: Include your contact information. If you do not have representation, then your contact information will be a phone number. Make sure you've got voice-mail hooked up. Casting offices are way too busy to keep phoning you with the hope you'll eventually pick up the call. If you do have representation, *do not list your personal contact information*; instead, list the contact information of your agent and/or manager.

An employer doesn't need to have your personal information until they book you for a job. Anyone who is professional in the business will always contact your agent or manager if he or she is interested in working with you. When a production tries to contact my client directly, I always get nervous because I feel like they're trying to hide something from me. And since my job is to protect the client and make sure that his or her best interests are being looked after, shady behavior like this puts up a red flag.

And whatever you do, don't lie on your resume. "It can be really embarrassing if the casting director you're reading for cast one of the projects on your resume and knows they didn't cast you in it," says Michelle Lewitt.

EXPERIENCE

The first category you list on a resume is experience. Of course, if you're just starting out, you may not have any experience. That's okay. You have to start somewhere.

This is where everything we discussed in chapter 2 comes into play. List school plays and community theater, student films, and shorts you starred in for your friends. List any work you did on local productions, even as an extra. The total sum of all of this experience might look impressive.

What you don't list on a resume are print jobs and commercials. However, you may put a section for commercials that notes "Conflicts available upon request." This means that at any given moment, I can rattle off your current conflicts so a casting director will know what products and services are still available for you to go out for.

CONFLICTS

In the world of commercials, you are generally only allowed to have one ad in each category running at any given time. For instance, if the category were fast food, you couldn't appear in both a McDonald's and Burger King commercial simultaneously. It might confuse consumers if they saw the same pitchman hawking hamburgers from two competitors. Besides, McDonald's probably doesn't want to invest a ton of money into someone who is advertising for their competitor at the same time.

Of course, you can have commercials running in multiple categories at the same time. In fact, I recently had a client who had six nationals running simultaneously in fast food, soft drinks, pastries, telecommunications, snack foods, and credit cards.

TRAINING

One of the first things casting directors will ask you when they meet you (especially when you're starting out) is, "Whom are you studying with?" When you're brand new, casting directors don't expect you to have a lot of experience, but they do expect to see that you're in class and perfecting your craft. Everyone has to start somewhere, and showing that you are serious about your training can go a long way in helping get you in the door. This is why listing training on your resume is so important.

Show a variety of training. Are you enrolled in a scene study class? Have you trained in improv? Audition techniques? Have you taken a commercial workshop? All of this is valuable and worth noting. Also, don't limit your training section to acting only. Do you work with a vocal coach? Have you taken dance lessons? Are you learning any musical instruments? All of this information should be listed in this section.

If you've studied theater at the university level, be sure to include this information as well. Casting directors hold high regard for actors who went to college to study their craft and graduated with a BFA in theater (see page 92). Many of these graduates are brought in for auditions based on the reputation of their school alone.

SPECIAL SKILLS

Another very important part of your resume is a list of your special skills—things you can do that make you unique. Can you sing? What is your range? Can you dance? What type of moves? Do you play any sports? Which ones? Are you fluent in any foreign languages?

Make sure you list your skill level as well. If you are just learning to play guitar, don't list it on your resume unless you notate that you are a beginner; otherwise, casting may call you in for a role that requires an expert guitarist and you won't be able to perform what they need.

Think outside the box. No matter how crazy or bizarre you might think your special skill is, you never know when there will be a need for it. Can you burp on cue? Can you make yourself cry? Can you fit your fist inside your mouth?

"Resumes should include skills that could possibly set you apart from the rest," advises Leder. "My client had ear wiggling on his resume. When Doritos wanted an expert ear wiggler for a commercial, he of course ended up booking the job."

Comp Cards

Comp cards, short for compilation cards, also known as *Zed cards*, are used primarily in the print and fashion industry. This card contains a compilation of shots of each model shown in different looks and styles. It also lists that model's measurements right on the card. Typically, there is a main photo on the front of the card and three or four additional looks on the back.

"A comp card is used as a marketing tool to get a model seen," explains Leza Labrador, director of Vue Model and Talent Agency. "They are also for the model to use as a leave behind, kind of like a resume, for an [advertising] client to refer to after the model has left."

In addition to comp cards, models will often bring their portfolios to *go-sees* (auditions, in model-speak). "A portfolio is a book of a variety of images, work, and tears," explains Labrador. "This is a model's bible. They bring this with them on castings to show the client a larger range of looks and the experience a model has."

Reel

As you start to book film and television jobs, you will want to put together a reel. A reel is a compilation of scenes from professional work you've done that can be used to show a casting director or agent your range as an actor. Like a resume, a reel should be updated constantly, whenever new footage becomes available.

Before you have footage to put on a reel, you'll just have to make do without one. Some actors like to record scenes or monologues, but this tends to come off as amateurish. Instead of helping you get a job, it just illustrates the fact that you haven't gotten a professional job yet. Student films and shorts that you make with your friends could go either way. If they come out looking professional and showcase your performance in a positive light, then clips of the work can be included on a reel. But if the production value is low and the work isn't flattering to your acting ability, it's better to refrain from including them. No reel at all is better than having one that doesn't sell you well.

You can hire one of many companies available to cut together your reel. Or, you can do it yourself and edit one on your personal computer. When you choose scenes for your reel, try to find ones that show a wide range of emotions. Even if all of your work comes from the same project, be sure to show different parts of the character you play. Find a scene where you're happy-go-lucky, then insert a scene where you're irate, and follow that up with one in which you're distraught. If that's not a tour de force, I don't know what is. Of course, you may not have that many options to choose from when you're starting out.

Keep the reel short, and put your most impressive stuff at the beginning. A casting director may not have enough time to watch the whole reel, so you want to make sure you put your best foot forward. A reel should typically be under five minutes long.

■ ■ ■

Remember, a great headshot will get you in the door. What you do in the room will determine whether you're invited back. Chapter 6 will explore what you need to do in the room to make a great impression. But first we'll explore what you can do while you're waiting for that next audition.

WHILE YOU ARE WAITING

James Immekus was an average student attending high school just outside of Atlanta. His Hollywood dreams were still a few years away. What he was starting to get into was drumming—specifically hand drums. One of his buddies was an expert drummer and showed his pal how to play.

Immekus picked up the instrument fairly quickly, and drumming soon became an avid hobby of his. Whether jamming with friends or thumping it out at home, Immekus enjoyed pounding out beats. Little did he know this skill would later come in handy.

CUT TO: Immekus was in Hollywood a few years later pursuing his acting career. He auditioned for the lead role in the movie *Boxboarders!* The character happened to be a drummer. While Immekus's acting chops ultimately won him the role, it certainly didn't hurt that he would actually be able to play the drums in the movie.

Having ancillary skills as an actor can be tremendously beneficial. This is why I always encourage my clients to learn as many unique skills as they can while they're pursuing their acting career. By the way, when you watch *Boxboarders!*, you'll notice Immekus on drums and another actor playing guitar. If you listen closely, the drums you hear are really Immekus playing, while the guitar from the other actor had to be dubbed.

An actor's life in between jobs is more than just a series of auditions and sitting around waiting for the phone to ring. At least it should be. This chapter explores how to effectively make acting your full-time job—on and off the set.

Journal

In most professions, you go to the office or a job site, work a set amount of hours, and then come home. With acting, there's no office to go to, and you must be self-disciplined so that you maximize your efforts. In essence, acting should be your full-time job. When you're actually on set or onstage, this concept is easier to grasp. But acting needs to be your full-time vocation even when you're not "working."

Here's an exercise I give my own clients: Get a notebook or journal and document how much time you spend working on your acting career every day for two weeks. Mark down auditions, classes, preparation, and anything else you do in a typical day that helps make you a better actor. Generally, I've found that the hours logged come up short. My clients find that they're spending nowhere near forty hours a week on their acting careers.

Sometimes they've got another job that gets in the way. But I remind them, "You didn't move to L.A. to wait tables." Whatever job you have should be secondary to your acting career. As I mentioned in chapter 2, it should provide enough money to pay your rent and bills, because it doesn't matter how many auditions you have—if your basic needs aren't met, you won't be able to focus well enough to book the acting gig.

Of course, kids who attend regular school may not physically have enough time to work on their acting career full-time. But it should be their top priority outside of school. If you need to choose between football practice and acting class, you should always choose the latter. But if your child would rather go to football practice (and there's nothing wrong with that), acting probably isn't his main passion, and this may not be the business for him. While I encourage my clients to do both, they have to find the right balance. In fact, I want well-rounded kids who have a complete life outside of the business. It makes them more real and, in essence, more marketable. But I still need to be sure that when push comes to shove, the career will prevail.

As for what to include in the journal, and how to fill up forty hours a week, read on. The remainder of this chapter will give you ideas and suggestions on how you can make acting your full-time job. After reading this chapter, document another two weeks in your journal. If you take my advice, I bet you'll find yourself working full-time on your acting career, and I guarantee your opportunities and productivity will increase.

Analyze This

Watch and analyze as many great performances as you can. Rent old movies. See current releases. Go to the theater. What did you like about the actors you saw? What didn't you like? Were they real? Believable? Did they connect with the audience?

Not sure where to start? Here are a couple of lists to give you some suggestions. First, I've included the American Film Institute's list of the Fifty Greatest American Screen Legends. Then I've included a list of actors who have won Oscars since the inception of the Academy Awards. Try putting together your own list of actors whom you admire and screen any of their work that you haven't yet seen.

AMERICAN FILM INSTITUTE'S LIST OF THE 50 GREATEST AMERICAN SCREEN LEGENDS

MEN

1. Humphrey Bogart
2. Cary Grant
3. James Stewart
4. Marlon Brando
5. Fred Astaire
6. Henry Fonda
7. Clark Gable
8. James Cagney
9. Spencer Tracy
10. Charlie Chaplin
11. Gary Cooper
12. Gregory Peck
13. John Wayne
14. Laurence Olivier
15. Gene Kelly
16. Orson Welles
17. Kirk Douglas
18. James Dean
19. Burt Lancaster
20. The Marx Brothers
21. Buster Keaton
22. Sidney Poitier
23. Robert Mitchum
24. Edward G. Robinson
25. William Holden

WOMEN

1. Katharine Hepburn
2. Bette Davis
3. Audrey Hepburn
4. Ingrid Bergman
5. Greta Garbo
6. Marilyn Monroe
7. Elizabeth Taylor
8. Judy Garland
9. Marlene Dietrich
10. Joan Crawford
11. Barbara Stanwyck
12. Claudette Colbert
13. Grace Kelly
14. Ginger Rogers
15. Mae West
16. Vivien Leigh
17. Lillian Gish
18. Shirley Temple
19. Rita Hayworth
20. Lauren Bacall
21. Sophia Loren
22. Jean Harlow
23. Carole Lombard
24. Mary Pickford
25. Ava Gardner

ACADEMY AWARD WINNERS
BEST ACTOR IN A LEADING ROLE

1927/28	Emil Jannings	*The Last Command* and *The Way of All Flesh*
1928/29	Warner Baxter	*In Old Arizona*
1929/30	George Arliss	*Disraeli*
1930/31	Lionel Barrymore	*A Free Soul*
1931/32	Wallace Beery	*The Champ*
	Fredric March	*Dr. Jekyll and Mr. Hyde*
1932/33	Charles Laughton	*The Private Life of Henry VIII*
1934	Clark Gable	*It Happened One Night*
1935	Victor McLaglen	*The Informer*
1936	Paul Muni	*The Story of Louis Pasteur*
1937	Spencer Tracy	*Captains Courageous*
1938	Spencer Tracy	*Boys Town*
1939	Robert Donat	*Goodbye, Mr. Chips*
1940	James Stewart	*The Philadelphia Story*
1941	Gary Cooper	*Sergeant York*
1942	James Cagney	*Yankee Doodle Dandy*
1943	Paul Lukas	*Watch on the Rhine*
1944	Bing Crosby	*Going My Way*
1945	Ray Milland	*The Lost Weekend*
1946	Fredric March	*The Best Years of Our Lives*
1947	Ronald Colman	*A Double Life*
1948	Laurence Olivier	*Hamlet*
1949	Broderick Crawford	*All the King's Men*
1950	José Ferrer	*Cyrano de Bergerac*
1951	Humphrey Bogart	*The African Queen*

1952	Gary Cooper	*High Noon*
1953	William Holden	*Stalag 17*
1954	Marlon Brando	*On the Waterfront*
1955	Ernest Borgnine	*Marty*
1956	Yul Brynner	*The King and I*
1957	Alec Guinness	*The Bridge on the River Kwai*
1958	David Niven	*Separate Tables*
1959	Charlton Heston	*Ben-Hur*
1960	Burt Lancaster	*Elmer Gantry*
1961	Maximilian Schell	*Judgement at Nuremberg*
1962	Gregory Peck	*To Kill a Mockingbird*
1963	Sidney Poitier	*Lilies of the Field*
1964	Rex Harrison	*My Fair Lady*
1965	Lee Marvin	*Cat Ballou*
1966	Paul Scofield	*A Man for All Seasons*
1967	Rod Steiger	*In the Heat of the Night*
1968	Cliff Robertson	*Charly*
1969	John Wayne	*True Grit*
1970	George C. Scott	*Patton*
1971	Gene Hackman	*The French Connection*
1972	Marlon Brando	*The Godfather*
1973	Jack Lemmon	*Save the Tiger*
1974	Art Carney	*Harry and Tonto*
1975	Jack Nicholson	*One Flew over the Cuckoo's Nest*
1976	Peter Finch	*Network*
1977	Richard Dreyfuss	*The Goodbye Girl*
1978	Jon Voight	*Coming Home*

Continued on next page

77

1979	Dustin Hoffman	*Kramer vs. Kramer*
1980	Robert De Niro	*Raging Bull*
1981	Henry Fonda	*On Golden Pond*
1982	Ben Kingsley	*Gandhi*
1983	Robert Duvall	*Tender Mercies*
1984	F. Murray Abraham	*Amadeus*
1985	William Hurt	*Kiss of the Spider Woman*
1986	Paul Newman	*The Color of Money*
1987	Michael Douglas	*Wall Street*
1988	Dustin Hoffman	*Rain Man*
1989	Daniel Day-Lewis	*My Left Foot*
1990	Jeremy Irons	*Reversal of Fortune*
1991	Anthony Hopkins	*The Silence of the Lambs*
1992	Al Pacino	*Scent of a Woman*
1993	Tom Hanks	*Philadelphia*
1994	Tom Hanks	*Forrest Gump*
1995	Nicholas Cage	*Leaving Las Vegas*
1996	Geoffrey Rush	*Shine*
1997	Jack Nicholson	*As Good as It Gets*
1998	Roberto Benigni	*Life Is Beautiful*
1999	Kevin Spacey	*American Beauty*
2000	Russell Crowe	*Gladiator*
2001	Denzel Washington	*Training Day*
2002	Adrien Brody	*The Pianist*
2003	Sean Penn	*Mystic River*
2004	Jamie Foxx	*Ray*
2005	Philip Seymour Hoffman	*Capote*

2006	Forest Whitaker	*The Last King of Scotland*
2007	Daniel Day-Lewis	*There Will Be Blood*
2008	Sean Penn	*Milk*

BEST ACTOR IN A LEADING ROLE

1927/28	Janet Gaynor	*7th Heaven, Street Angel,* and *Sunrise*
1928/29	Mary Pickford	*Coquette*
1929/30	Norma Shearer	*The Divorcee*
1930/31	Marie Dressler	*Min and Bill*
1931/32	Helen Hayes	*The Sin of Madelon Claudet*
1932/33	Katharine Hepburn	*Morning Glory*
1934	Claudette Colbert	*It Happened One Night*
1935	Bette Davis	*Dangerous*
1936	Luise Rainer	*The Great Ziegfeld*
1937	Luise Rainer	*The Good Earth*
1938	Bette Davis	*Jezebel*
1939	Vivian Leigh	*Gone with the Wind*
1940	Ginger Rogers	*Kitty Foyle*
1941	Joan Fontaine	*Suspicion*
1942	Greer Garson	*Mrs. Miniver*
1943	Jennifer Jones	*The Song of Bernadette*
1944	Ingrid Bergman	*Gaslight*
1945	Joan Crawford	*Mildred Pierce*
1946	Olivia de Havilland	*To Each His Own*
1947	Loretta Young	*The Farmer's Daughter*
1948	Jane Wyman	*Johnny Belinda*

Continued on next page

1949	Olivia de Havilland	*The Heiress*
1950	Judy Holliday	*Born Yesterday*
1951	Vivien Leigh	*A Streetcar Named Desire*
1952	Shirley Booth	*Come Back, Little Sheba*
1953	Audrey Hepburn	*Roman Holiday*
1954	Grace Kelly	*The Country Girl*
1955	Anna Magnani	*The Rose Tattoo*
1956	Ingrid Bergman	*Anastasia*
1957	Joanne Woodward	*The Three Faces of Eve*
1958	Susan Hayward	*I Want to Live!*
1959	Simone Signoret	*Room at the Top*
1960	Elizabeth Taylor	*Butterfield 8*
1961	Sophia Loren	*Two Women*
1962	Anne Bancroft	*The Miracle Worker*
1963	Patricia Neal	*Hud*
1964	Julie Andrews	*Mary Poppins*
1965	Julie Christie	*Darling*
1966	Elizabeth Taylor	*Who's Afraid of Virginia Woolf?*
1967	Katharine Hepburn	*Guess Who's Coming to Dinner*
1968	Katharine Hepburn	*The Lion in Winter*
	Barbara Streisand	*Funny Girl*
1969	Maggie Smith	*The Prime of Miss Jean Brodie*
1970	Glenda Jackson	*Women in Love*
1971	Jane Fonda	*Klute*
1972	Liza Minnelli	*Cabaret*

1973	Glenda Jackson	A Touch of Class
1974	Ellen Burstyn	Alice Doesn't Live Here Anymore
1975	Louise Fletcher	One Flew over the Cuckoo's Nest
1976	Faye Dunaway	Network
1977	Diane Keaton	Annie Hall
1978	Jane Fonda	Coming Home
1979	Sally Field	Norma Rae
1980	Sissy Spacek	Coal Miner's Daughter
1981	Katharine Hepburn	On Golden Pond
1982	Meryl Streep	Sophie's Choice
1983	Shirley MacLaine	Terms of Endearment
1984	Sally Field	Places in the Heart
1985	Geraldine Page	The Trip to Bountiful
1986	Marlee Matlin	Children of a Lesser God
1987	Cher	Moonstruck
1988	Jodie Foster	The Accused
1989	Jessica Tandy	Driving Miss Daisy
1990	Kathy Bates	Misery
1991	Jodie Foster	The Silence of the Lambs
1992	Emma Thompson	Howards End
1993	Holly Hunter	The Piano
1994	Jessica Lange	Blue Sky
1995	Susan Sarandon	Dead Man Walking
1996	Frances McDormand	Fargo

Continued on next page

1997	Helen Hunt	*As Good as It Gets*
1998	Gwyneth Paltrow	*Shakespeare in Love*
1999	Hilary Swank	*Boys Don't Cry*
2000	Julia Roberts	*Erin Brockovich*
2001	Halle Berry	*Monster's Ball*
2002	Nicole Kidman	*The Hours*
2003	Charlize Theron	*Monster*
2004	Hilary Swank	*Million Dollar Baby*
2005	Reese Witherspoon	*Walk the Line*
2006	Helen Mirren	*The Queen*
2007	Marion Cotillard	*La Vie en Rose*
2008	Kate Winslet	*The Reader*

BEST ACTOR IN A SUPPORTING ROLE

1936	Walter Brennan	*Come and Get It*
1937	Joseph Schildkraut	*The Life of Emile Zola*
1938	Walter Brennan	*Kentucky*
1939	Thomas Mitchell	*Stagecoach*
1940	Walter Brennan	*The Westerner*
1941	Donald Crisp	*How Green Was My Valley*
1942	Van Heflin	*Johnny Eager*
1943	Charles Coburn	*The More the Merrier*
1944	Barry Fitzgerald	*Going My Way*
1945	James Dunn	*A Tree Grows in Brooklyn*
1946	Harold Russell	*The Best Years of Our Lives*
1947	Edmund Gwenn	*Miracle on 34th Street*

1948	Walter Huston	*The Treasure of the Sierra Madre*
1949	Dean Jagger	*Twelve O'Clock High*
1950	George Sanders	*All About Eve*
1951	Karl Malden	*A Streetcar Named Desire*
1952	Anthony Quinn	*Viva Zapata!*
1953	Frank Sinatra	*From Here to Eternity*
1954	Edmond O'Brien	*The Barefoot Contessa*
1955	Jack Lemmon	*Mister Roberts*
1956	Anthony Quinn	*Lust for Life*
1957	Red Buttons	*Sayonara*
1958	Burl Ives	*The Big Country*
1959	Hugh Griffith	*Ben-Hur*
1960	Peter Ustinov	*Spartacus*
1961	George Chakiris	*West Side Story*
1962	Ed Begley	*Sweet Bird of Youth*
1963	Melvyn Douglas	*Hud*
1964	Peter Ustinov	*Topkapi*
1965	Martin Balsam	*A Thousand Clowns*
1966	Walter Matthau	*The Fortune Cookie*
1967	George Kennedy	*Cool Hand Luke*
1968	Jack Albertson	*The Subject Was Roses*
1969	Gig Young	*They Shoot Horses, Don't They?*
1970	John Mills	*Ryan's Daughter*
1971	Ben Johnson	*The Last Picture Show*
1972	Joel Grey	*Cabaret*

Continued on next page

1973	John Houseman	*The Paper Chase*
1974	Robert De Niro	*The Godfather: Part II*
1975	George Burns	*The Sunshine Boys*
1976	Jason Robards	*All the President's Men*
1977	Jason Robards	*Julia*
1978	Christopher Walken	*The Deer Hunter*
1979	Melvyn Douglas	*Being There*
1980	Timothy Hutton	*Ordinary People*
1981	John Gielgud	*Arthur*
1982	Louis Gossett Jr.	*An Officer and a Gentleman*
1983	Jack Nicholson	*Terms of Endearment*
1984	Haing S. Ngor	*The Killing Fields*
1985	Don Ameche	*Cocoon*
1986	Michael Caine	*Hannah and Her Sisters*
1987	Sean Connery	*The Untouchables*
1988	Kevin Kline	*A Fish Called Wanda*
1989	Denzel Washington	*Glory*
1990	Joe Pesci	*Goodfellas*
1991	Jack Palance	*City Slickers*
1992	Gene Hackman	*Unforgiven*
1993	Tommy Lee Jones	*The Fugitive*
1994	Martin Landau	*Ed Wood*
1995	Kevin Spacey	*The Usual Suspects*
1996	Cuba Gooding Jr.	*Jerry Maguire*
1997	Robin Williams	*Good Will Hunting*
1998	James Coburn	*Affliction*
1999	Michael Caine	*The Cider House Rules*
2000	Benicio del Toro	*Traffic*

2001	Jim Broadbent	*Iris*
2002	Chris Cooper	*Adaptation*
2003	Tim Robbins	*Mystic River*
2004	Morgan Freeman	*Million Dollar Baby*
2005	George Clooney	*Syriana*
2006	Alan Arkin	*Little Miss Sunshine*
2007	Javier Bardem	*No Country for Old Men*
2008	Heath Ledger	*The Dark Knight*

BEST ACTRESS IN A SUPPORTING ROLE

1936	Gale Sondergaard	*Anthony Adverse*
1937	Alice Brady	*In Old Chicago*
1938	Fay Bainter	*Jezebel*
1939	Hattie McDaniel	*Gone with the Wind*
1940	Jane Darwell	*The Grapes of Wrath*
1941	Mary Astor	*The Great Lie*
1942	Teresa Wright	*Mrs. Miniver*
1943	Katina Paxinou	*For Whom the Bell Tolls*
1944	Ethel Barrymore	*None But the Lonely Heart*
1945	Anne Revere	*National Velvet*
1946	Anne Baxter	*The Razor's Edge*
1947	Celeste Holm	*Gentleman's Agreement*
1948	Claire Trevor	*Key Largo*
1949	Mercedes McCambridge	*All the King's Men*
1950	Josephine Hull	*Harvey*

Continued on next page

1951	Kim Hunter	A Streetcar Named Desire
1952	Gloria Grahame	The Bad and the Beautiful
1953	Donna Reed	From Here to Eternity
1954	Eva Marie Saint	On the Waterfront
1955	Jo Van Fleet	East of Eden
1956	Dorothy Malone	Written on the Wind
1957	Miyoshi Umeki	Sayonara
1958	Wendy Hiller	Separate Tables
1959	Shelley Winters	The Diary of Anne Frank
1960	Shirley Jones	Elmer Gantry
1961	Rita Moreno	West Side Story
1962	Patty Duke	The Miracle Worker
1963	Margaret Rutherford	The V.I.P.s
1964	Lila Kedrova	Zorba the Greek
1965	Shelley Winters	A Patch of Blue
1966	Sandy Dennis	Who's Afraid of Virginia Woolf?
1967	Estelle Parsons	Bonnie and Clyde
1968	Ruth Gordon	Rosemary's Baby
1969	Goldie Hawn	Cactus Flower
1970	Helen Hayes	Airport
1971	Cloris Leachman	The Last Picture Show
1972	Eileen Heckart	Butterflies Are Free
1973	Tatum O'Neal	Paper Moon
1974	Ingrid Bergman	Murder on the Orient Express
1975	Lee Grant	Shampoo

1976	Beatrice Straight	*Network*
1977	Vanessa Redgrave	*Julia*
1978	Maggie Smith	*California Suite*
1979	Meryl Streep	*Kramer vs. Kramer*
1980	Mary Steenburgen	*Melvin and Howard*
1981	Maureen Stapleton	*Reds*
1982	Jessica Lange	*Tootsie*
1983	Linda Hunt	*The Year of Living Dangerously*
1984	Peggy Ashcroft	*A Passage to India*
1985	Anjelica Huston	*Prizzi's Honor*
1986	Dianne Wiest	*Hannah and Her Sisters*
1987	Olympia Dukakis	*Moonstruck*
1988	Geena Davis	*The Accidental Tourist*
1989	Brenda Fricker	*My Left Foot*
1990	Whoopi Goldberg	*Ghost*
1991	Mercedes Ruehl	*The Fisher King*
1992	Marisa Tomei	*My Cousin Vinny*
1993	Anna Paquin	*The Piano*
1994	Dianne Wiest	*Bullets over Broadway*
1995	Mira Sorvino	*Mighty Aphrodite*
1996	Juliette Binoche	*The English Patient*
1997	Kim Basinger	*L.A. Confidential*
1998	Judi Dench	*Shakespeare in Love*
1999	Angelina Jolie	*Girl, Interrupted*
2000	Marcia Gay Harden	*Pollock*
2001	Jennifer Connelly	*A Beautiful Mind*
2002	Catherine Zeta-Jones	*Chicago*

Continued on next page

2003	Renée Zellweger	Cold Mountain
2004	Cate Blanchett	The Aviator
2005	Rachel Weisz	The Constant Gardener
2006	Jennifer Hudson	Dreamgirls
2007	Tilda Swinton	Michael Clayton
2008	Penelope Cruz	Vicky Cristina Barcelona

TV Junkie

A lot of parents won't let their kids watch too much television. Grandma used to always say, "TV rots your brain." But watching television shows that are currently in production is an integral part of your job.

I always say to watch every show at least one time. If you have an audition for that show, it is imperative that you be familiar with it. Know the characters, the setup, and the pacing. Being familiar with these variables can give you a competitive edge over other actors who are up for the same job.

There's a big difference between how you will approach a role on a one-hour drama (which is like acting in a film) and one on a sitcom (which is all about the timing). There's an even bigger difference if that sitcom were on Disney Channel or Nickelodeon, where the acting tends to be bigger and broader than a half-hour show on ABC or CBS. And every show within each format has its own idiosyncrasies. The quick repartee on *Gilmore Girls* is quite different from the slow and steady pacing of *Law & Order*. Know and understand the nuances that differentiate one show from another. The best way to become familiar with the acting on each show is to watch each show.

Classes, Coaching, and Preparation

I've said it before, but I'll say it again. Being in an ongoing acting class is vital to success in this business. After all, acting is a muscle. And going to class is like going to the gym. The more often you work out, the bigger your muscles get. The more often you work your acting muscle, the better your craft will be.

If an audition comes up and you've been working your acting muscle on a regular basis, you're going to go into the casting office confident and prepared. However, if it's been a few weeks, or a few months, since the last time you picked up a script and worked on copy, you're probably not going to fare very well. Get into the habit of regularly exercising your acting muscles. The best way to do this is to attend an ongoing class.

Acting coach Dennis LaValle has worked with some of the top young actors in Hollywood, including Shane West, Gregory Smith, and Gabrielle Union. "Any actor who wants to 'make it' in this town needs to study," says LaValle. "It's called 'show business,' and you have to do whatever you can to give yourself an edge on the competition.

"I get calls from agents and managers all the time checking up on their clients to see how they are progressing and to make sure that they are working at their craft," LaValle continues. "They want to see if their clients are working as hard for their careers as they are. They want to be sure that when that actor goes in for the audition they do a good job because they are not only representing themselves but the agency that sent them. In a sense, every time an actor reads for a role he is representing the kind of talent that comes out of the agency or management company that sent him.

"From a sheer craft point of view, studying can be one of the greatest joys of an actor's life," says LaValle. "It's a fellowship and a sense of artistic community that can fill a performer up with inspiration, hope, and strength that he or she needs to survive."

Michelle Lewitt of the Casting Company says it's important to switch it up a bit. "Being with the same class for five years may get you into a plateau or comfort zone that affects your growth as an actor," she says. "Don't be afraid to challenge yourself with something new. You will only benefit from it."

In chapter 3, I discussed the benefits of working with an acting coach before a major audition. But some people prefer to work privately with a coach on a regular basis as well. While this may be more costly than being in a class, the one-on-one training can be extremely beneficial.

Every actor has her own coaching needs. Acting coach Tanya Berezin finds that for emerging actors, their concentration is sometimes in the wrong place. "What do I do? How do I give it to them? How do I book a job?" Berezin queries. "With coaching, my approach is, 'How do I do it as if I've already booked the job?'"

Berezin helps the more advanced actor own the role and show casting something specific to him that no one else has shown. "I ask the actor a series of questions that they forget to ask themselves so that the uniqueness of the character is revealed," says Berezin. "Actors must bring 100 percent of themselves into an audition, but sometimes they start to take things for granted instead of being in the moment."

Whatever you do, however you do it, make sure you spend enough time preparing for each audition. If you want to just go in and wing it, consider all of your competition that has been working on the material since the moment they received it. Who do you think will make a better impression in the room?

Maximize whatever time you have available to prepare for your audition. You have plans for dinner? Cancel them. You've got to work? Call in sick. If you're not prepared for an audition, don't bother going. You will likely harm your chances if the casting director sees you stumble through copy. You won't be doing anyone a favor by showing up unprepared.

Is it possible to over-prepare? Absolutely, so be careful. You want your audition to feel genuine and spontaneous when you're in the room. Over-prepared, over-rehearsed actors can sabotage their auditions when their read feels regurgitated from too much practice. But most actors can gauge when they're ready to rock. This skill will come with time.

"When younger performers over-prepare they are less likely to be able to 'unfreeze' their performance and take direction or make new choices as they simply don't have the experience to do so," reveals LaValle. "In addition, over-preparation does not allow for the actor to understand that they can do everything right in an audition and still have the powers-that-be want to 'see it another way.' This can be confusing as the actor may feel that they have failed or really messed up their audition and then have that thought confirmed because they are so locked into their performance that they can't make any adjustments."

TOP UNIVERSITY THEATER PROGRAMS

Going to a four-year college program for theater can give some actors a leg up in Hollywood. Casting directors know, by the very reputation of the schools themselves, that graduates of these theater programs are generally well trained and ready to book professional jobs. While it's not necessary to attend a university theater program to become an actor, it's certainly a viable option.

Carnegie Melon
www.cmu.edu/cfa/drama

Cincinnati Conservatory of Music
www.ccm.uc.edu/drama/curric_frameset.html

DePaul University
theatreschool.depaul.edu/schoolmain.php

Juilliard
www.juilliard.edu/college/drama/programs/index.html

Northwestern
www.communication.northwestern.edu/departments/theatre/programs.php

New York University
drama.tisch.nyu.edu/page/home.html

University of California at Los Angeles
www.tft.ucla.edu/programs

University of Michigan
www.music.umich.edu/departments/theatre/programs.htm

University of Southern California
theatre.usc.edu

Yale University
drama.yale.edu

Working with Scene Partners

When you are in a scene study class, you're typically assigned a partner and given a scene to work on. Of course, not all the work takes place in the class. You need to meet several times outside of class to really nail the material.

Just because a scene isn't assigned to you by an acting coach, it doesn't mean you can't get together with other actors and work on scenes in a non-classroom environment. In fact, I encourage my clients to do this.

Not sure what to work on? Choose material that you might be auditioning with. Ask your representatives for sides from current TV shows. Ask your acting coach to suggest some plays to work on. You can even work together on actual auditions.

LaValle recommends starting a play reading group at your house. "Choose a different play every week," he advises. "Read it, cast it, and then get together as a group and do a staged reading in your living room. This speaks to the 'fellowship' that I mentioned earlier. You can make it into a weekly ritual, brunch, picnic, or even dinner party. It bonds actors and gives you a sense of empowerment that is hard to come by unless your name is Brad or Angelina."

Reading List

If you're reading this book, then there's a good chance you're already engaged in this next activity. Read. Read scripts. Read plays. Read books about acting—both the craft and the business. The more you read, the more you can learn about the industry that we're all in.

You can find most film scripts on the Internet. Many popular ones are also published, so check out sites like amazon.com to see what you can find. There's also a defunct magazine called *Scenario* that used to publish complete screenplays. You can still find old copies online.

You should also read stage plays. The best collection in L.A. is located at Samuel French Bookstores. In New York, check out the Drama Book Shop. Not in either of these cities yet? Order from them online. From the classics to modern theater, you should be well versed in this literature and constantly looking for roles you can play.

PLAY SCRIPT SOURCES

Samuel French: www.samuelfrench.com

The Drama Book Shop: www.dramabookshop.com

Playscripts, Inc.: www.playscripts.com

Reading about the business you are in is very useful. You can always learn something new from every book you read. Read how-to books, books about the entertainment industry, and actor biographies.

Finally, stay up-to-date on the business by reading trade publications. *Daily Variety* and *The Hollywood Reporter* are the best periodicals about industry news. *Backstage* magazine is a must read for every actor in town. You can get online subscriptions to all of these magazines as well. There are also several other websites where you can get news that pertains to the industry.

TRADE PUBLICATIONS

Backstage: www.backstage.com

Billboard: www.billboard.com

The Hollywood Reporter: www.thr.com

TV Week: www.tvweek.com

Variety: www.variety.com

Self-Submission

Just because you don't have representation, it doesn't mean you can't submit yourself for certain projects that are casting. And just because you do have representation, it doesn't mean you should stop submitting yourself on certain projects. Let me explain.

Everybody works as a team. When you sign with an agent or manager, that doesn't give you a license to sit back and wait for the phone to ring. You should continue to work as hard as ever. Your representation gives you a certain level of credibility in this business, so it should help in your own efforts to secure a job.

Many sites allow actors to submit their headshots and resumes for casting opportunities without the help of an agent or manager. You can sign up for free accounts on sites like Now Casting, Actors Access, and LA Casting, where you can browse through breakdowns and casting notices and send in your headshot and resume with a few clicks of the keyboard. And you can subscribe to *Backstage*, which also publishes casting notices.

"Submit on anything and everything that you are right for," advises manager Bryan Leder. "But be honest and be realistic about what you play, and don't submit on a role unless you plan on working it if you get booked."

A few words of caution about self-submitting: "Talent needs to be careful about submitting themselves on Internet projects [typically low to no-budget, *non-union* webisodes]," warns agent Vivian Hollander. "As long as [the project] can be verified as reputable, it can provide experience." If you're ever unsure, it's probably a good idea to pass on the project. If you don't get a good feeling about the people involved, or you're questioning the content of the piece itself, move on. There will be other opportunities out there.

You should also be cautious when self-submitting on non-union jobs, which means they are not regulated by the Screen Actors Guild and don't have to adhere to SAG rules such as meal breaks and work hour restrictions (see page 98 for a discussion of unions). However, they still must adhere to labor laws. Educate yourself about those laws so that you know what your rights are. Since a studio teacher might not be present on a non-union set, parents will have to pay a lot of attention to safety issues surrounding their children working on such a project.

CLICK TO SUBMIT

Actors Access: www.actorsaccess.com

Now Casting: www.nowcasting.com

LA Casting: www.lacasting.com

Backstage: www.backstage.com

Practice and Experience

Experience is the name of the game when you're starting out. Get it wherever you can, and start to build your resume. Jump on any opportunity you can find to work as an actor, no matter how big or small, no matter if it doesn't pay much or doesn't pay at all. The only way to become a better actor and build a resume is to get experience.

Investigate student films. There are great film schools in L.A. and New York, not to mention all over the country, and these student filmmakers need actors to appear in their projects. Some of the films turn out amazing and can actually be used on clients' reels. In fact, when I sign new developmental clients, I strongly encourage them to do student films to get started, although I try to steer them more toward graduate level films that tend to have higher production values.

"Starting out having tape on a client is huge," says manager Jamie Malone. "I have put together great reels from footage from student films, allowing me to get the client paying jobs and better representation."

"I had two clients in an AFI [American Film Institute] film that was being cast by a well-known casting office," reveals manager Bryan Leder. "They hadn't worked with these actresses before. But after, they were brought back to that casting office on many other professional projects. You can build relationships everywhere."

Both coasts also have an abundance of ninety-nine-seat theaters. These are smaller theaters that will cast both union and non-union actors for plays that tend to have a limited run. Being in a play six nights a week is the only thing better than going to acting class. I strongly encourage my clients to do any theater they can, because I know they'll be working their acting muscles on a regular basis during the run of the show. I do caution parents to make sure they read and are comfortable with any material they have their children audition for. And since most theater is performed at night, your days will still be free for auditioning and booking film and television work.

Want to take a more aggressive approach? Make your own short films. If you're not having any luck getting cast in someone else's project, take matters into your own hands and put together a short that will showcase you as an actor. You don't need to spend a lot of money; just grab some friends, come up with a script, and start shooting. Not only will you have fun in front of the camera, but you'll also get a glimpse into moviemaking, which will help you better understand the process.

Getting into the Unions

The two main unions for film and television are the Screen Actors Guild (*SAG*) and the American Federation for Television and Radio Artists (*AFTRA*). SAG covers most films and television shows that are shot on film. AFTRA covers most taped shows and radio work. Actors *Equity* Association (AEA) is the union that covers theater. Every actor worries about how he or she will get into the unions. After all, you must be in a union to book a union job. But if you're a non-union actor, how can you get in? Clearly, a challenging catch-22 situation exists.

There is a process called *Taft-Hartley* that allows a production to tap a non-union actor into the union. Not every production likes to do this as it costs extra money to hire a non-union actor for a role, but it is done—more often than you might think.

When casting a role, producers want to find the absolute best person for the job. Sometimes that person may be non-union. In such cases, they will gladly Taft-Hartley the non-union actor so that he or she can play the role. But study hard and perfect your craft. I've never had a problem getting one of my non-union clients a job on a union project. But when it happens, it's usually for a significant role like a guest star on an *episodic* or a large supporting role in a feature film. There are so many union members who aren't working that it's more difficult to hire a non-union actor for a smaller part.

Actors should also be cautioned against joining the union too soon. Once you become a union member, you are no longer eligible to do non-union work. As such, joining a union prematurely could hinder your career.

After an actor does her first union job, she becomes *eligible* to join the union. The actor can work two more union jobs before she must join the union. I always suggest that my clients hold off on joining the union until they become a *must join*.

Extra Work

Working as a *background* actor, or extra, is a great way to get on location so that you can observe what it's like to be on a living, breathing set. Productions need background actors of all ages. Smart extras take note of everything that's going on around them so that they can learn about production and prepare themselves for when they're cast in their first speaking role on a show.

But be careful. You don't want to overstep your boundaries. You are there to perform an important function. Speak to the crew when spoken to, but this is not your opportunity to pass out your headshot. On screen, extras are seen, but not heard. The same should be true off screen.

There are some additional benefits to doing extra work. A certain number of background actors must be members of SAG. For full-budget features, the first fifty extras must be SAG, and on low-budget features, the first thirty extras must be SAG. For television, the first *stand-in* and nineteen extras must be SAG.

After that, producers can hire non-union extras. If for some reason the production fails to provide the required number of SAG extras, non-union extras will be used in their place and they will earn a SAG voucher. Once a non-union extra earns three SAG vouchers, he will be eligible to join the union.

In addition, some extras are able to get upgraded to an under-five player if they're given lines. This automatically makes you eligible to join the union. It is generally the *assistant director* who chooses which non-union extras will be upgraded with a SAG voucher. The director generally decides to give a line to a background actor. In either case, being punctual and professional at all times will certainly make you a stronger contender than someone who shows up late or sits on set and complains all day. So while I wouldn't make a career out of doing extra work, I do think there's much to be gained by testing the waters.

Actor Rocky Marquette has starred in dozens of movies including *Shallow Ground, Mortuary*, and *1968 Tunnel Rats*. But when he first moved to L.A. from Michigan, he started his career as a background actor.

"I went to Central Casting to sign up and they take your picture and get your sizes and put you in their database," explains Marquette. "That night you can start calling the information line to see if they are casting your type. If they are, you call into that casting person and leave your ID number and they call you back with a *call time* if you fit the description."

Marquette's intention was to work as an extra until he could collect his three SAG vouchers so he could get into the union. But he was lucky. His cousin worked on *The Ellen Show* as a hairdresser. "She talked to Ellen who then talked to the second AD [assistant director] and they got me my vouchers," reveals Marquette. "I had to work three days in order to get them, one voucher each day, but I got them and joined SAG right away.

"Doing background work really helped me out a ton when I first moved to L.A.," says Marquette. "I was very green when it came to film and TV acting. I had no idea how a set worked or the lingo that they used. But I learned very fast. I loved it and it helped me learn how a real production worked."

Another early triumph for the young actor was when he got a call from Central Casting to go to Sony Studios to meet Sam Raimi, director of the *Spider-Man* films, to see if he approved of Marquette to be Tobey Maguire's *photo double*. Raimi looked at him and said, "Wow, you look just like Tobey." Marquette was hired instantly and worked as Maguire's stand-in on *Spider-Man* for two months.

"I would encourage any new actor who is totally green to try out background work and get a feel for how a production runs," advises Marquette. "If you are lucky, you might get into the union, make cool new friends, and meet some amazing actors."

EXTRAS CASTING COMPANIES

Here is a list of some extras casting companies on both coasts.

LOS ANGELES

> **Sandra Alessi Casting**
> www.sandealessicasting.com
>
> **Bill Dance Casting**
> www.billdancecasting.com

NEW YORK

> **Grant Wifley Casting**
> www.gwcnyc.com
>
> **Extra Talent Agency**
> www.extratalentagency.com

BOTH LOS ANGELES AND NEW YORK

> **Central Casting**
> www.centralcasting.org

Working Out and Staying in Shape

Physical fitness can play a vital role in determining whether you book jobs. That isn't to say that people who are not in shape can't book jobs—in fact, there are great character actors who are super-thin or overweight. But if you are a leading man or leading lady, you probably want to live an active lifestyle, and fitness should become part of your everyday routine.

If you're playing high school, you don't want to bulk up too much. I don't know too many muscleheads who are sixteen years old. Instead, stay lean and toned. You want to look good in a bathing suit, but you don't want to look like a bodybuilder.

If you've never worked out at a gym before, think about getting a personal trainer—at least at the beginning. Having a professional show you how to properly lift weights can help prevent you from accidentally hurting yourself. If you can't afford a trainer, partner up with a buddy who can help spot you and guide you through a basic workout. And parents, kids should stay active by playing sports, swimming, and riding their bikes. They do not need to be in a gym pumping iron!

Self-Promotion

Another thing you can be doing is spending time each week promoting yourself. Think of it as being your own publicist . . . until you can afford one, of course. And given that you are the product, there's always something to promote.

When you're just starting, you might want to do mailings of your headshot and resume to agents and managers if you're seeking representation, or to casting directors for whom you would like to audition. Now that you've got great promotional tools, professional reps and casting directors need to see them. However, blind mailing can get costly, so some may opt to wait until you've got an actual project to promote. Others, rather than sending headshots, will print postcards that are easier (and cheaper) to mail.

If you're doing a play, appearing as a guest star in a television show, or have a film opening, these are all good reasons to do an industry mailing to make them aware of what you're up to. If you're looking for new representation, then target agents and managers. If you're just looking for more casting opportunities, target the casting community.

"With the Internet now, every casting director has a business e-mail address," says Harriet Greenspan, who has cast such shows as *True Jackson, VP* as well as the pilot for *Drake & Josh*. "I think the best thing to do is e-mail. Mailing can be quite costly. Also, so many casting directors constantly move offices, but most people don't change their e-mail like they do their office address. When your child does something spectacular, or the first thing they do, I think it's a good idea to tell a casting director. People e-mail me, and I always answer them."

The Savage Agency owner Judy Savage also agrees that e-mail or mailings are best when you have something to say. "'Watch me on this show on this night.' Or, 'Thank you for casting me in this show,'" says Savage. "Casting directors get so much mail, so make sure it's something really unusual."

"We're more likely to bring someone in from a mailing commercially, more so than theatrically or for voice-over," says CESD's Melissa Berger. "But if we do, we'll meet them with an eye toward other fields of representation as well."

Breakdown Services (the company that releases breakdown notices exclusively to talent reps) also publishes a book with the contact information for all casting directors. The Hollywood Creative Directory publishes a book that lists all agents and managers. Samuel French sells preprinted labels for both!

TO BE, OR NOT TO BE . . . PREPARED

If you still have time to fill and you want some other activities, try these suggestions from acting coach Dennis LaValle.

» Study Shakespeare, see Shakespeare, read all the plays, rent all the movies, and go to as many Shakespeare productions as you can, because when you study the best you become the best.

» Take ballroom dance, hip-hop, ballet, swing, tap, and salsa.

» Adults can learn how to fire a handgun, shotgun, or bow and arrow.

» Learn how to ride a horse, use a sword, and do martial arts.

» You should be able to do at least five different accents!

"In short, prepare for the audition that may require one of these skills tomorrow, next week, or next year," says LaValle. "Prepare for the audition that you don't have yet, and then when it comes you won't have to do a crash course in any of the above."

■ ■ ■

If you catch yourself wondering what you could be doing for your acting career again, reread this chapter. There are so many ways to propel your career—you should be racking up overtime. Of course, as soon as that audition comes up, all resources should be redirected to preparing for that meeting. The next chapter will walk you through a typical audition.

THE AUDITION

Austin Basis began his acting career in New York when he finished college. He signed with a talent manager who sent him for an audition to be a series regular on a new pilot for NBC. He was excited, though nervous, as this was only his second audition ever. The project was called *Spellbound*, and it was a half-hour comedy about a female mortal who falls in love with a male witch. Austin would read for the role of the witch's brother. He thought his audition went well, but he didn't hear anything back.

A week later Basis received a call telling him that the studio was going to fly him to Los Angeles to test for the role in the pilot. Only Austin and one other actor passed the studio test at Warner Bros. The network test for NBC was later that day. On his way home from the second test, he got a call telling him that he didn't get the part. Basis had a long flight back to the East Coast.

While NBC had made the pilot, it was never picked up. A year later, the property was owned by Fox and Basis was asked to come back and read for the same part. He auditioned again, and again they wanted to test him. But due to their tight schedule, there wasn't enough time to fly Basis to L.A. for the studio test. Instead, they would just screen the tape from his audition with casting.

Basis wasn't crazy about the idea of auditioning on tape while the other actors would have the opportunity to audition in person. Nonetheless, his tape passed the studio test and, immediately, he was flown to L.A. on a red-eye to come to the network test the next day. When Basis arrived at LAX the next morning, he retrieved his voice-mail only to discover that the network test was cancelled because they were having trouble finding their other actors.

In August, Basis got another call, letting him know that they had finally found the lead actor, a pre–*Brothers & Sisters* Dave Annable, with whom they were going to have Basis read. They wanted to fly Basis back to L.A. once more for yet another round of studio and network tests. He passed the studio test for the third time and then went to the network test at Fox.

Basis felt like he had nailed it. It turns out that everyone loved him, but the head of the network at the time wasn't 100 percent convinced that Basis was the guy. So they decided to wait a month to see if they could find anyone else who was better and then retest Austin against the new choices.

A month later, back in New York, Basis received another call telling him they wanted to fly him to L.A. that night. They were going to test the role the next day and if he got the part, the ***table read*** would take place two days later.

They tested Basis against one other actor. The minute he left the audition, the network head gave her approval, and he finally landed the job! Two days later, they filmed the pilot. Basis was on his way.

Auditioning all those times for the same role can really make an actor second-guess himself. "You need to find new ways to make it fun and funny," says Basis. "That way, it's always fresh when you walk in the room."

After all that, the pilot never got picked up. But it was an experience Basis will never forget, and with the money he made shooting the pilot, he was able to pack up and move to L.A. He also signed with his first agent as a result of the pilot and he's been working nonstop ever since.

■ ■ ■

When my clients go to an audition, all I want them to do is walk in the room and do great work. Let me worry about everything else. This chapter reveals the secret for giving a great read and making a great impression. It's not just about what happens in the room. It starts with proper preparation and ends with an analysis of your feedback. But it also includes such underestimated considerations like waiting room etiquette, *threshold skills*, and casting director chitchat.

Where Do Auditions Come From?

Typically when a project is casting, the casting director will release a list of characters with descriptions of each role she needs to cast. This list is called a breakdown. Agents and managers subscribe to Breakdown Services and submit their clients who they feel best match each part.

Sometimes casting directors will look through the headshots and resumes to determine which actors they would like to see for each role. Other times, agents and managers will call a casting director on the phone and pitch each client they have submitted. Because so many actors are submitted for each role, this personal "push" can be effective in securing the actor's appointment.

Casting director Lauren Bass says there is a key to making a successful pitch call. "For a pitch call to be effective, it is helpful if the agent or manager has actually read the script and understands the character that I am seeking," she says. "Additionally, it is important for the rep to really know the client and his or her capabilities. That way we can have a discussion about the 'essence' of the character and how the specific actor may or may not fit the role."

PRE-AUDITION MATERIALS

Once an audition is scheduled, your agent or manager will phone you with the details. At Management 101, we follow up this call with an e-mail. This e-mail contains an appointment sheet, a copy of the original breakdown, the sides, and a script.

The appointment sheet has pertinent information on it like the name of the project and the role you will be reading for. It also has the date and time of the audition, the name and title of whom you will be reading for, the location of the casting office, and any special notes that are pertinent to the audition (such as how you should dress, which gate to drive to on the studio lot, or how "big" to make the character).

The breakdown will have a description of the character you are reading for. It might also describe some of the other characters in the piece and present a short summary of the film or TV show. Read this information carefully, because it could give you additional insight into your character. The breakdown will also list additional players involved with this project like producers, the director, and the studio, network, and/or production company.

Sides is a fancy word used to describe audition copy. Typically, these are one or two scenes from the screenplay that showcase the character you are reading for. Feel free to mark them up, highlight your lines, and make any notations on them you need to. You will study these sides to prepare for your audition, and you will bring them into the audition room in case you need to reference them.

Whenever a full script is available, we always send that along to our clients as well. Reading the entire screenplay before entering an audition room allows the actor to learn so much about the character that he may not glean from just scanning the sides. However, scripts for high-profile movies might not always be available because the producers want to avoid leaking any information to the press. Episodic TV scripts are constantly being rewritten, so you'll seldom get to read those prior to the audition. In fact, by the time you book the job and get to set, episodic sides have typically changed completely from what you saw when you first auditioned.

Your agent and manager work very hard to get you auditions—calling casting directors to convince them you are right for a certain role and urging them to see you—so do whatever you can to get there on time and enter prepared. Remember, for every audition you have, there are probably a thousand other actors who didn't get this opportunity. That is why you want to go into the room and put your best foot forward each and every time.

The Lobby

The audition starts the moment you enter the building. You never know who might be roaming the hallways, so always be on your best behavior. You don't want a *casting associate* to pass you in the hall as you're screaming into your cell phone at the pal you're fighting with or your ex-girlfriend. If you're a parent accompanying an unruly child, you certainly don't want a *casting assistant* spotting Mom in full reprimand mode. The audition has begun. Everyone you come in contact with could be a person who helps you or your child get this job. So just act professionally.

When you enter the casting office you need to put your name on the sign-in sheet. The casting director will generally see people in the order they arrive. If you have representation, put their information on the sign-in sheet where it asks for a phone number. If you don't have representation, put your cell number down. Be sure to give the correct information, as these numbers will be used to alert you of a callback.

SIGN OUT

It's equally important to sign out of an audition. In fact, many actors forget to do this simple task. Believe it or not, not doing so could cost you money!

There's a little-known union rule that states that if you're at an audition for more than an hour from your time of arrival, or if you are called back for a third or subsequent audition, you will be paid a fee. Casting directors are required to submit their sign-in sheets to the union upon request, and the only way to prove the length of your audition is if you have signed in and out.

As you sit in the waiting room, focus on getting in character. It's not a time to **network** with the other actors or exchange gossip with the other mothers. Everyone is there for the same reason—so that they (or their kid) will book the job. Do you really think the competition wants you (or your kid) to book the job over them? While they may appear friendly at first, they could be trying to get information out of you to help themselves, or they might be feeding you with misinformation to psyche you out. Better to just focus on the task at hand and keep to yourself.

Once your name is called, enter the audition room right away. Don't tell the casting assistant that you need to finish your phone call. Don't be wandering down the hallway out of earshot from the person who is announcing that your turn has come. Chances are they've got a busy schedule with lots of people to see. Even though they may have kept you waiting, it is not okay to keep them waiting.

Pre-Read

A *pre-read* is the first audition you have with casting. It's a chance for a casting director to get to know a new actor, or an opportunity for her to see if an actor she knows would be right for a particular role. It is your opportunity to make a great impression on the casting director so that she decides to give you a callback where you will audition for the producers.

Some actors don't like pre-reads, especially if they're with a casting office that already knows them well. They'd rather go straight to producers. And, as your career continues to grow, and you consistently prove yourself in audition rooms and collect more fans, the reality is that you will begin to bypass pre-reads and meet directly with producers. In fact, once you become a bona fide star, you may bypass auditions altogether because you'll be receiving straight offers.

But as I stated earlier, a casting director can be your best friend. The reason I like pre-reads is because it's not just an opportunity for the casting director to see you read; it's also a chance to work with you and give you adjustments so that you can give the producers exactly what they want to see in the callback.

"The pre-read is often an important stepping stone to the producer session," says casting director Lauren Bass. "I do a lot of work with actors during pre-reads. In some cases, they are more like coaching sessions. If an actor has 'something,' but isn't necessarily hitting all the right marks, I will use the pre-read to encourage him to explore the role further in order to discover different facets of the character. That is an opportunity that one might not be afforded in a producer session."

Do you need to be *off-book* in a pre-read? Sometimes that's just impossible. With commercial casting, you typically don't receive the material in advance, so they tend to function as cold reads. With theatrical appointments, you generally have more time with the material, so you could prepare the scene adequately and be off-book when you go in. But it is not imperative to be off-book. It is imperative not to rely too heavily on the copy, however. You want the casting director to see your face and reactions, and that might not be possible if your nose is in the script the entire time you're in the room. You should be so innately familiar with it that you can deliver it naturally, as if you've already been hired and the cameras are rolling on set. Remember, confidence books the job.

"[The term] 'off-book' is misleading," says Bass. "It's not enough to simply memorize lines. I'm not interested in regurgitation of dialogue. I believe one should instead opt for familiarizing himself with the dialogue—get it into his body, his voice ... become comfortable with the material so it becomes second nature and conversational."

In addition to the casting director, there could be a few other people in the room when you audition. There will always be a *reader*, who reads the copy opposite you. Sometimes this is the casting director or one of her associates. There may also be a camera operator in the room who will run the video camera that puts you on tape.

Sometimes the casting director isn't even in the room at all. Instead, she may have her associate run the session and put everyone on tape. They can go through the tape at a later time to determine which auditions they want the producers to look at.

There are all types of readers. Some will read with you and give you a great performance to work off of. Others will give you nothing but a droll emotionless line read. No matter how the reader delivers his lines, don't let him throw you. You always need to give 100 percent back.

Many different things could happen in the room. Just go with the flow and be flexible. On some occasions, you might have been told to only prepare one scene, but now they want to see you read another. This is probably a good sign, so put your cold read skills to work. In other instances, you might have been told to prepare all scenes, but when you arrive they alert you that you'll only be reading the first scene. Don't let this throw you, and don't overanalyze the situation. The reason this happens may be as simple as they're running behind and just don't have enough time to have everyone read all scenes.

If a casting director gives you an adjustment, or notes on your performance, listen to what she says and don't be afraid to ask questions or for clarification. Being given direction is typically a good sign because it indicates that the casting director liked something about your read and wants to see if you're consistent, or can take direction, or if you can nail the part with the right guidance.

If you're not asked to read the scene again, don't worry about this too much, either. You may have just hit it so well the first time that they don't need to see you do it again. Sometimes my clients will come out of a casting office thinking they blew the audition because they only did it once, and the next thing you know they're getting a callback.

You may find that casting directors will want to chitchat with you before or after your audition. This is their chance to get to know you a little better as a person and out of character. If you are engaged in conversation, this is another chance for you to shine. Be charming and confident and real. If they really like you as a person, it could be enough to turn a "maybe" into a callback.

Feedback

I try to get feedback on auditions whenever I can. It's the only way my clients can learn and grow and become better actors. However, for a variety of reasons, I can't always get the feedback I'm seeking. The casting office may be too busy. With most commercial auditions, they're simply searching for a look. Whatever the case may be, just know that we always try to get feedback because it also helps us do our job better.

As soon as your audition is through, you should touch base with your representation to let them know how you thought it went. This will always trigger me to put in a call to casting to get their feedback. But hearing my client's version of the audition will also give me insight into understanding casting's response. Having heard both sides of the audition story, I can make more sense out of what happened in the room.

"Feedback from auditions is a wonderful tool for agents and managers to gauge exactly what level our clients are at," says agent Julie Fulop. "It can help us to guide them in the direction needed as far as training. Do they need to improve their improve skills? Do they need to work further on emotion? Were they too reserved or too over the top in their read?"

"It's also a great tool to help actors see how casting views their choices," says manager Jamie Malone. "It will explain what is not working, allowing us [the team] to make adjustments to help you book the next job. It also gives us a list of casting fans we can go back to and remind them of you to get more opportunities."

Sometimes I get feedback and it's just not helpful. "They did a good job, but we have stronger choices"; "We just didn't respond"; "It was interesting, but not going further." This doesn't help my client or me at all. So I try to dig a little deeper and get something specific and constructive out of them. Sometimes casting directors just don't like giving bad feedback. But when they do, it can really help an actor correct problems that may be occurring and help him grow as a performer.

When I call for feedback, I generally want to hear one of two things. Either, "She got the job!" or, "She didn't get the job, but I loved what she did in the room, and we will definitely be bringing her back in the future." What I don't want to hear is "She is still very green," or, "She came in unprepared." These comments tell me you didn't do your homework. When your agent and manager are busting their butts to get you into every room, you want to make sure that you do your part and hit a home run every time.

Actors need to listen to the feedback without getting defensive. You must also understand that there are some things that you have absolutely no control over no matter how good a job you did. "She was too tall"; "She was too short"; "He was too good-looking"; "He wasn't good-looking enough . . ." No matter the comment, I've heard them all before. Don't take any of them personally. The right role will come along. In the meantime, if you make a great impression every time you go in because the work is strong, whether you are right for each particular job or not, you'll always be invited back.

For example: Ben McKenzie had only been in Los Angeles for a year when he tested for his first pilot. The Texas native was up to play the boyfriend of the lead girl on a new show for UPN. He went through the testing process and it came down to Ben and two other actors. The tapes were sent off to the head of the network and word came back that they decided to go with a person of color for that role.

"I have range, but not that much range," jokes McKenzie.

Warner Bros., the studio that was producing that show, really liked McKenzie's read. The moment he was released from his **test deal**, they auditioned the young actor for another show that they were producing. Within a week, he tested for this new show and got the role.

"This was an even better show with an even better role for me," recalls McKenzie. "It worked out magically."

The new show was *The OC*, and it made McKenzie a household name. Subsequently, the UPN pilot was shot but never picked up. Not only that, UPN no longer exists. As for McKenzie, he continues to work, most recently as a series regular on *Southland* for NBC.

Callback

Congratulations! You got a callback. You should be proud of yourself, because getting a callback is a surefire sign that you did a great job in the room. When a casting director gives a callback, she stakes her reputation on the actor. Essentially, she's telling her boss, the producer, that she thinks any of the actors she called back would be great for the job. It's now up to the producers to make the final decision.

Whatever you did in the room when you first went in obviously worked. It got you a callback. So unless the casting director gives you specific notes to alter your read, go back and do exactly what you did the first time. Of course, if the producers give you adjustments in the room, follow their lead. But otherwise stick to the way you did it originally.

Also don't change what you were wearing in the pre-read. Maybe that shirt made you look a little younger? Maybe the skirt made you seem a little taller? Whatever the case may be, dress exactly the same. Now is not the time to start changing things up. If it ain't broke, don't fix it.

A NOTE ABOUT WARDROBE FOR AUDITIONS

For film and television auditions, actors should dress casually, with small accents hinting at what their character may dress like. In other words, if you are auditioning for the part of a baseball player, you don't have to put on a uniform, but a cap might be a good idea. For commercial auditions, the casting director generally will spell out the type of wardrobe required, such as playground casual or back to school attire, based on the product.

"Keep it simple," advises Bryan Leder, founder of Bryan Leder Talent. "Unless the role is specific, wear simple clothes that bring out your eyes and complements your skin tone."

In all cases, stay away from logos or anything too tight or too baggy. Also, kids should not accessorize. "A girl came in to sing for me and her earrings were so big and heavy," recalls Leder. "It was so distracting that to this day I can't remember the song that she sang or what she looked like. But I do have clarity on the earrings."

Casting director Michelle Lewitt hates when actors change something in a callback. "Don't ever do this," she warns. "If you got a callback, it's because we liked what you did in the room. Nothing ruins a callback more than an actor who left my pre-read session, over-thought the scene or character, deduced his own changes, and came back in with something *totally* different. Unless we tell you to change something, when you come back, do it like you did the first time!"

Lauren Bass says the most common mistake an actor makes in a callback is getting in his own way. "Sometimes for a pre-read, the actor feels less pressure, so he's more himself. Then the callback comes and all of a sudden, the nerves and the anticipation of getting the job cloud the way he behaves in the room. All the work on the character and the material flies out the window."

Of course, if you receive a callback, you should probably be as close to off-book as possible. "For a producer's session, I can't imagine why you wouldn't want to be off-book," suggests Lewitt. "Even if you still have the pages in your hand for reference, in the event the producer or director gives you notes and you want to visually see where you're going to make the adjustments, you should still know the scene very, very well."

For most costar and guest star roles on episodic television and most supporting roles in films, you will learn if you booked the job soon after the callback. The audition process is over. However, there are some instances where you may have to audition again.

Maybe you get a second callback because the producers aren't 100 percent sure which way they want to go, so they invite their top choices back into the room for one last look. Maybe you get called back for a different role because you did a great job, but the producers think you might be better suited to play another character. Or maybe you get a second callback because not all of the producers were in the room the first time, or they want the director to see you as well before making their final decision. Whatever the case may be, bring it completely every time you go back into the room.

Testing

For series regulars in television shows and leads in certain movies, the callback with producers is typically only the second step in the auditioning process. You still have another round or two of auditioning left. Of course, each time you move up a rung, your competition lessens.

In television, the producers' choices for their series regulars must audition for the studio that is producing the series as well as the network that is airing the show. This process is known as testing. Before an actor tests for a series, he or she must sign a test deal.

Test deals are contracts between an actor and the studio that outline all of the parameters of each party's responsibilities and obligations. The agreement will include how much an actor is paid for the pilot as well as an episodic fee. It will list the term of the contract, determine the billing, and state the actor's degree of exclusivity to the project. All actors who test for a show must sign the deal before they test. Studios do that for leverage so that they don't make their choice and then have to negotiate a contract after the fact.

Before a test there is typically a *work session*. In most instances the session is run by the director or casting director. It is an opportunity to work on the role a bit more intensively. It can give the director a chance to direct your performance for the test so that he can showcase you in what he feels is the best possible light.

Sometimes the studio and network tests are combined. This is most common when the studio and network are the same. But more often than not, the studio test comes first. Then, those actors who pass the studio test will proceed to the network test. The second test may be the same day, or it may not happen for another week.

In both cases, be prepared to see a lot of executives in the room. Don't let this throw you off. In addition to the casting director, producers, and director, there will also be studio and network casting directors, and development and *programming executives*. Unless you were given specific notes to follow and incorporate during the work session, just follow the advice from the original callback—don't change a thing.

Generally, each actor will be called in one at a time and then be asked to wait in the lobby until all the actors for each role have been seen. Sometimes certain actors will be asked into the room more than once. Don't get nervous if this is you, and don't be upset if it isn't you. When an actor is asked to come back into the room, it could be for a number of reasons. Sure, maybe this actor is the choice and they want to see her one more time just to be sure. Or maybe this actor split the room—some of the executives loved her, and others didn't get her at all, so they're bringing her back for another shot. Still, maybe they have a new note for the actor who they brought back in and they want to see if she can make the adjustment.

You can really go crazy overanalyzing why they bring you back in, so the best way to proceed is to not worry about it. If you just do a great job every time you are in the room, and you always bring your A-game to the table, you can't go wrong. The rest is left up to fate.

A mix-and-match session is when actors playing different roles are paired up to read together. Producers want to see who looks best side by side, or which couple has the best on-screen chemistry. Always give your scene partner everything you've got, because that's what you would like back in return.

After a test, the executives will decide which test deal to execute, and in doing so, the actor is hired. However, sometimes after a test is finished, the executives decide to go back to the drawing board and start from scratch again because they didn't feel that any of the final choices presented the perfect fit for the role. So if you're ever in a situation where you're not testing against anyone else, don't be too cocky. There's still a good chance you might not pass the test and the executives will go back to square one.

General Meetings

Another type of audition that actors should be familiar with is the *general meeting*. General meetings are typically held with casting directors or *casting executives* on the studio or network level, but they can also be with a director, producer, or other studio or network executive. Their purpose is for the person you are meeting with to get to know you.

The reasons behind general meetings vary. Perhaps someone saw you perform and is now a fan of your work and wants to learn a little more about you, to find ways to put you in projects she's involved with. Maybe your agent or manager introduced you to a casting executive at one of the studios by way of your reel, and now this person is excited about the "new actor" he discovered. Whatever the reason, it's a great opportunity for you to sit one-on-one with an industry professional and sell yourself in the room.

You may be asked to read copy in a general meeting, but not always. Instead, look at it as an opportunity for someone to get to know you better. As such, your personality and charm need to shine.

Don't be shy or demure. Go in there and light up the room. Be fun. Be funny. Ask questions. Make a connection. If you sit on the couch with not much to say, you'll only bore the person to tears. If she leaves the meeting feeling like she was pulling teeth just to get you to talk, it probably isn't a good sign.

"General meetings are basically just to give us an idea of who you are as a person, but it is not a substitute for your work, or craft," says the Casting Company's Lewitt. "I'm usually wowed after the fact, when I've met them, then look at their reel, and realize they've really got range because the roles they've played are nothing like the person that sat in the chair in front of me. Go in, be yourself, be genuine, and let them see who you are."

"Most casting directors don't like to do generals because they get a better idea of a person's talent when they're reading them for a specific project," reveals casting director Harriet Greenspan. However, when she does take a general meeting, she looks for specific qualities. "I look for energy, sense of humor, and personality (how vivacious they are). So much of the actor's real personality goes into the role they play. So many roles are geared toward their personality. Once the writer gets to know you, they actually write for you."

Greenspan also warns against being disingenuous. "Do not come in to kiss my butt," says Greenspan. "Just be someone who can talk about yourself and show me who you really are."

Threshold skills are those traits an actor must call upon when you walk into a room. From the moment you enter the office, you are on. If you're having a bad day, or you just found out some exciting news, you have to leave it all behind and focus on the task of making a new fan.

Do your homework before you go in. Get online and Google the person with whom you are meeting. Find out what projects he's worked on and whom you might know in common. Get information on the projects he has coming up that you might be right for.

At the same time, make sure you educate the person about you. Where are you from and how did you get to Los Angeles (or New York, or whatever the case may be)? How long have you been acting, and where do you study? What have you worked on, and what were those experiences like? Fun anecdotes and funny stories always seem to go over well. What kinds of roles would you like to play in the future?

Not all actors, as brilliant as they may be, are very good in a room, and as such, I don't recommend general meetings for everyone. For kids, especially, general meetings are difficult. What is a seven-year-old going to talk about with the head of the studio? And not all casting directors like to take general meetings. Some would prefer just to meet the actors through their work. That said, if you find yourself lucky enough to have a general meeting, just go in confident and prepared. Don't try too hard to be something you're not. Instead, let them be charmed by your engaging personality. Make a great impression, and the benefit could last a lifetime.

■ ■ ■

Now that you've nailed the audition, get it out of your head. If you keep wondering whether you booked the job, you will drive yourself crazy. Just relax knowing that you gave it your all and if it's meant to be, you'll be hearing from them soon.

BOOKING THE JOB

Shane Harper was never looking to get into show business. In fact, the young performer only picked up dancing because he was bored waiting in the lobby while his sister took her classes. So he decided to bide his time by enrolling in class as well.

A few years later, when he was thirteen, Harper was competing in a dance competition. An agent saw him and signed him—and that's how he got his start. But he didn't go into the business intentionally. It was always just something to do for fun.

Soon after he signed with the agent, his family went on a camping trip to Santa Barbara. His dad had just spent five hours setting up the campsite when their cellphone rang—Shane had his first audition.

The family was supposed to be gone for four days. But this audition was the next day. So the Harpers sat together and discussed how much time and energy they were willing to give to this new venture.

The next morning, shortly after waking, the family packed up their campsite and drove their Airstream trailer to L.A. They had to stop for clothes so that Shane would have something appropriate to wear for the audition.

That first meeting was for *Reanimated*, a live-action movie for Cartoon Network. And, would you believe, he booked the job. "That confirmed for our family that we had made the correct choice," says Harper. "We knew we were in this for the long haul."

Subsequently, Shane booked his next two auditions as well. He's been going strong ever since, appearing in projects such as *High School Musical 2* and *Zoey 101*, and as a series regular on Nickelodeon's *Dance on Sunset*.

■ ■ ■

Congratulations, you booked a job. Now it is time to solidify your relationship with the people who hired you and use this momentum to book your next gig. But it isn't all wine and roses. In addition to these important topics, we'll also discuss the very real issue of dealing with rejection and how to keep your head up when the business keeps knocking you down.

Avails

Sometimes producers will narrow down the field to include just their top couple of choices. Perhaps they need network approval on a major recurring guest star role. Maybe they don't have their shooting schedule set in stone yet, so they can't officially make an offer because they don't know how long that role will work. To protect themselves from the actor accepting another job, they put that actor on *avail.*

Putting an actor on avail basically means that the office that makes the avail wants to be notified immediately if any other offers come in for the actor. They don't want to lose the actor to another project, so they ask for this professional courtesy. Sometimes this is called putting an actor on hold, or putting a pin in an actor.

It's quite possible to be put on avail and then never book the job. In one example, the casting office may put their top two choices on hold in case they couldn't work out the schedule with their first choice . . . but since they were able to close that deal, you would no longer be on hold. In a second case, perhaps you had a pin in you for an episode of *Lost*, but they ended up cutting the role from the script. Regardless of the reason why you were put on avail but still didn't book the job, just know that you got very close, and, like a callback, this is a true sign that whatever you're doing is working correctly.

Let's Make a Deal

Once the production works out their schedule, they are ready to make an offer. For most jobs, the terms are fairly standard. They include the actor's fee, time commitment, billing, and dressing room. For larger jobs like leads in films and series regulars, additional terms may include publicity obligations, exclusivity, and profit participation, to name a few.

Most actors when starting out are paid scale plus ten. *Scale* is the minimum required payment as set forth by the actors' unions. The *plus ten* represents the commission an agent would receive when his or her client books a job. When an actor is paid scale plus ten, the agent payment is included on top of the actor's salary (in this case, scale), rather than deducted from the actor's salary. However, if you also have to pay a manager, that commission will be deducted from the scale amount.

As we discussed in chapter 5, there are two main unions that cover television: SAG and AFTRA (see page 98). SAG jobs tend to pay more than AFTRA jobs. But for some reason, most children's programming works on AFTRA contracts. Most features and TV shows that are shot on film are covered by SAG, while those projects shot on videotape are covered by AFTRA. Equity is the union that covers professional theater. Fees vary based on the size of the role you play. Once you build a resume, TV shows are sometimes willing to pay an actor above scale. This pay hike can be negotiated by your agent.

The production budget determines which contract is used for a feature film. The main contracts include the "ultra-low budget agreement," the "modified low budget agreement," the "low budget agreement," and the "SAG basic agreement." Once you build a resume, your agent can negotiate over-scale payments. While you may not be making the $20 million a picture that Tom Cruise receives, your quotes will eventually rise. After all, Tom Cruise didn't get $20 million on his first film.

There are different fees based on the amount of time you work. In television, costar roles command either daily or weekly rates; one-day or multi-day guest star roles will earn you varying rates as well. Per SAG, if an actor is a guest star on a series, and the role works for more than one day, then the actor must be paid *"top of show."*

MONEY MONEY MONEY

Considering that the minimum wage is $7.25 an hour (as of July 2009), the money you can make as an actor is quite good. Under the SAG basic agreement, a day player on a SAG project will make a minimum of $759 for the day. If the actor is employed on a weekly contract, he will earn a minimum of $2,634 for the week. In television, if the actor receives guest star billing, he must work either one day at a negotiated rate for no less than scale ($759), or he can work more than one day for no less than top of show. Top of show for half-hour programs is $4,080. Top of show for one-hour programs is $6,527. Actors will also receive *residual* payments for work that is re-aired.

Feature films are divided into four separate contracts by budget. For any budget over $2.5 million, the above rates apply. Under the low budget agreement, for films under $2.5 million, actors will receive a day rate of $504, and a weekly rate of no less than $1,752. Under the modified low budget agreement, for films with a budget less than $625,000, actors will receive a day rate of $268, and a weekly minimum rate of $933. Under the ultra-low budget agreement, for films with a budget of less than $200,000, actors will receive a day rate of $100.

AFTRA contracts typically pay less than the SAG basic agreement. In addition, this union negotiates specific rates with each individual show they cover. Cable shows tend to pay less than shows on major networks. AFTRA also has a much more lenient residual policy, allowing networks to re-air shows multiple times before any additional payment is due to the actors.

The term "top of show" comes from billing because most guest star roles receive their credit at the beginning of the episode, or top of show. However, most half-hour programs put their guest star billing in the end credits. Costar credit generally appears in the end credits regardless of show length.

In film, you want your credit to appear in the *main titles.* Main titles are generally at the start of the film, but sometimes a director will elect to put all the credits at the end of the film. When main titles appear at the end of the film, they are the credits that run immediately upon the film's conclusion. Smaller movie roles are typically credited in the cast crawl, which always comes at the end of the movie.

The other factor that goes into credit determination is whether the actor will receive a single card or a shared card. A single card has no one else's name on screen when the actor's name appears. A shared card will put two or more actor's credits on screen at the same time. If the card is shared, you want to limit the number of other performers who will appear on the same card as best you can. I also try to negotiate for top or bottom placement since these positions tend to stand out a little more.

Dressing facilities are the final factor to consider when making a deal. On some low budget films, you're lucky to get a dressing room at all. But typically, dressing rooms consist of a trailer when you're on location or a small room if you're working on a sound stage. As we discuss on page 149, there are several types of trailers. *Honey wagons* are the smallest trailers, followed by *triple bangers, double bangers*, and a *star wagon.* As your star rises, so will the size of your trailer. When it comes to my clients, I'm not so concerned with the size of the trailer, although bigger is generally better. However, I try to ensure that the trailer is private (meaning they don't have to share with another actor) and exclusive (meaning no one else will be using the trailer when my client isn't working).

Thank-Yous

Not everyone does this, which is exactly why you should: When you get cast in a role, send a thank-you note to the casting director. He or she has clearly become a fan and hopefully will continue to cast you throughout your career. In fact, I see that happen all the time with my own clients. Certain casting offices always bring back specific actors to read and cast them in roles again and again.

This business is built on relationships, so a small token of appreciation like a thank-you note can go a long way. That said, if you book a major role, like a lead in a film or a series regular on a pilot, you might want to consider sending a gift basket or flowers. This type of generosity will keep you in their thoughts at all times. Of course, you don't want to go overboard, either. It's truly the thought that counts, and any grandiose gestures could possibly be misconstrued and backfire.

Building Momentum and Booking the Next Job

Every time you book a job, you're not only expanding your resume, but you're also building your momentum in the business. Your agent and manager suddenly have something brand new to add to their pitch about you when they're on the phone with casting directors. "Jimmy is on fire lately. He just booked a guest star role on *CSI: Miami*!"

I always say that work begets more work. When you book a job, working will reinvigorate you. I've never met a client who didn't admit the thrill of being on set. The end of a shoot is always the hardest part of the job. An almost subconscious effort forms within the actor at his next set of auditions because he wants more than anything to be back on set doing what he loves to do.

Booking a job gives your team new fodder to talk about when pitching you to casting offices. "I can't boast about callbacks, close shots, or being second choice," jokes manager Bryan Leder. "When I'm pitching a client on a project, nothing speaks louder than what the client has recently booked. It's the best marketing tool that we've got. How many times have I tried to get a client into a specific office? All of a sudden they are interested in seeing that client now that there's some heat on her because she's just booked a role in another project. I laugh because to me she's always been fantastic even before she booked that role."

And of course, there's also the ancillary benefit of actually working every day. And that is, of course, the fact that you are stretching your acting muscle on a regular basis, as we talked about earlier in this book. Having the opportunity to work with other great actors and production personnel will also help you strive to do your best work.

Rejection

We've talked a lot about booking the job in this chapter, but it's equally important to discuss the ramifications of not booking the job. I read somewhere that it takes an average of sixty-one auditions until an actor books a job. Of course, I've had clients who have booked their first audition out of the gate, and I've had others who took longer than sixty-one opportunities to book. I suppose it all averages out in the long run.

When you go through a streak where you are not booking, it can be one of the most frustrating feelings in the world. If you're doing everything you should on your end, you can't beat yourself up. Sometimes actors don't book jobs for reasons that are completely beyond their control.

The key is to be consistent. Continue to give your best read each and every time you walk into the audition room. Monitor your feedback closely and embrace any and all constructive criticism you receive—it will only help you get better. Most of all, stay focused on the goal. Don't be distracted by the business around you. Let your reps worry about that. Instead, channel all of your energy into the work at hand.

Agent Melissa Berger helps her clients deal with rejection by making them focus on the positive. "It gives them a sense of perspective," says Berger. "They need to have a solid confidence and faith base—maybe this isn't the right one, but the right one is out there. You can't go into the room with desperation. You have to be here for the long haul. Having other interests outside the business also helps. You have to have a life."

"I have a saying: Interviews are like buses. If you miss one, there's another one along in twenty minutes," says agent Judy Savage. "You can't put all of your hopes in that one interview. You can't think of it as personal. You have to be tough. It's hard for kids. On the other hand, kids get rejected in school. My grandkids are in their school choir. They try out for solos and they get hurt when they don't get them, but they try out again and again. When a boy asks a girl out in high school, she might say no. All through life, someone gets a better job than you. Rejection is a part of life."

"With most of the guest star roles I've gotten, I've been told by the casting directors that at first glance I wasn't right for the role, that they had somebody else in mind," admits James Immekus, an actor who has appeared on dozens of shows, including *Cold Case*, *The Cleaner*, *Grey's Anatomy*, and *House*. "But if you can go in there and believe you're the best and be the best in the room, you can get the part despite that. Talent can win over looks."

Whatever you do, don't psyche yourself out. Don't overanalyze what you did or didn't do, or what you could or couldn't do better the next time. Don't look around the waiting area wondering if your competition is better looking. Just go in and do great work. Eventually, it will pay off.

"To be rejected means that you were in the game," says manager Bryan Leder. "There are so many actors trying to make it who aren't even in the game yet. Don't let minor setbacks like not booking a particular job overshadow the accomplishment of how far you've actually come."

Parents have a very important role when it comes to helping their child actors deal with rejection. Just be supportive of your kids. Let them know it's okay to not book the job. Continue to encourage them to strive for greatness. But also let them know that booking the job isn't everything. At the end of the day, be there to root them on, and also be there to comfort them when things aren't always going their way.

In essence, be a great parent. Their agent and manager can talk to them about feedback. Their coach can speak to them about the craft and how they can do better in the room. Parents, just be parents—leave the business talk to the professionals who are handling your child's career.

Sometimes rejection is just another step that brings you closer to your main goal. Asher Book had been working at his acting career for a few years. When he graduated from high school, he decided to take time off from acting to pursue his musical ambitions, so he joined the band V Factory as their lead singer. Even though he was focused on his music, he told his manager that if something special came along, he would audition for it.

Something special did come along. MGM was remaking *Fame* and they needed a good-looking male lead who could act and sing. It was Asher's dream role.

Asher went through the routine casting process. After a nationwide search, the studio decided to test a small handful of hopefuls for the role of Marco. Asher did a screen test and felt good about his performance. In fact, out of all the candidates, he was the only one they were holding. Everything looked like it was going his way.

But as the expiration date of his test deal quickly approached, the studio was hesitant to execute the contract. They weren't convinced Asher was their guy, and they wanted to keep looking. The contract lapsed and Asher was crushed.

While it wasn't completely over for Asher, this clearly wasn't a good sign. He immersed himself in his music and continued to rehearse with his band, trying not to think about his misfortune. Then things got worse. The trades announced that the star of *Terminator: The Sarah Connor Chronicles*, Thomas Dekker, was cast in the role of Marco. Fade to black.

But life has a strange way of working sometimes. Fox, the network that airs Dekker's show, picked up the series for more episodes. The revised production schedule conflicted with the shooting schedule for *Fame*. And, like that, Dekker was out of the movie.

So where did this leave Asher? His manager campaigned heavily for the studio to reconsider him for the role. The film's producer was also on board. But the studio continued to release breakdowns and search for alternatives. Finally, the studio agreed to retest Asher for the role.

This time, Asher tested against only one other candidate. He felt confident and invigorated to have this second chance. Lightning must have struck, because as soon as he finished testing, the producer told Asher he had booked the role.

■　■　■

Of course if all goes as planned, like Asher Book, you managed to book the job. Soon you will arrive on set for your first day of shooting. In the next chapter, we'll discuss what happens on set so you can prepare for your big day.

ON THE SET

Jodi Caldwell was on the set of *The Bernie Mac Show* with her son Andrew when he was guest starring on the popular Fox sitcom. Andrew was playing a high school wrestler alongside series regular Jeremy Suarez (Jordan Thomkins). This episode took place in the high school gymnasium during a wrestling match and called for a large number of background actors who were all dressed in wrestling singlets, just like the two boys.

It was taking a long time to set up a certain shot so Jodi and Andrew went to get something to eat. As they were about to enter the craft services room, someone from production told them that they weren't allowed to have any snacks—it was off limits to the extras. And while Jodi tried to explain that her son wasn't an extra, the production rep wasn't interested. Jodi did what any good stage mother should do. She called me, Andrew's manager, and told me what had just occurred.

I was on the tarmac of Bob Hope Airport in Burbank, having just landed, when I received her call. I left word with the producers to call me but figured it would be much easier to just swing by the set on my way to the office and speak to them in person. CBS Radford Studios, where they shot the show, was just about fifteen minutes from the airport.

I drove onto the lot and ran over to the set where I quickly found my client and his mom. They still hadn't shot anything, and the Caldwells still hadn't had anything to eat or drink. I asked one of the PAs to bring me to the producer, to whom I proceeded to explain what had happened. The producer quickly apologized, blaming the mistake on the large number of similarly dressed extras who were on set that day. She then apologized to my client and his mom as we all walked to craft services together and made some sandwiches.

In the end, everything worked out fine. The client and his mom did the right thing by avoiding confrontation with the production staff and letting me handle the problem. It was fairly easy to solve, but if someone had to be the bad guy, then it would have been me. If the producers got upset, they would get angry at me because we removed the client and his mom from the situation.

"Frederick always tells us, if there's ever a problem or a question, to call him first," explains Jodi Caldwell. "That way, Andrew can be there to focus on his work, and Frederick can handle any issues that arise. When I'm on set, I try to stay back and out of the way."

■ ■ ■

It is amazing to me how many talent reps help their clients book their first jobs and then throw them to the wolves without even the shortest orientation. This chapter explores what to expect when you arrive on set for the very first time. We'll also cover what your employers should expect from you.

Preproduction

Once you book a job, several things may happen. Depending on how quickly the production is commencing, some of these tasks may occur at lightning speed, in due time, or not at all. All of these activities that take place prior to filming fall into the area of *preproduction*.

Most people don't envision actors to be too essential during film prep once the casting process is completed. Instead, they're on their own, working on their lines and getting into character. But depending on the timeline, production needs, and budget constraints, actors could find themselves with a lot to do.

Wardrobe may call to set a time for you to go in and get measured. Or, they may just call and ask for your current sizes. Moms, make sure you own a measuring tape as kids' sizes change frequently. Sometimes you might have to visit the costume designer more than once. Subsequent visits are generally afforded so you can try on the clothes and the producers can see how you look in your costume. On some productions, the timeline between getting cast and working on set is so tight that there simply is no time for a *fitting*.

Lead actors in feature films are often asked to take part in a filmed hair and makeup test. Like a fitting, this is an opportunity for the producers to see what their actors will look like once they are all done up. Any time a major change to an actor's appearance is required for a role, there's a strong chance she'll be asked to do a hair and makeup test. Drastically changing hair length, altering hair color, or applying special effects makeup to create alien creatures are all likely reasons producers would want a test before filming.

Speaking of creatures, sometimes a lot of preproduction work involves creating molds and masks for the actors portraying these out-of-this-world roles. In such instances, the actor will meet with the special effects makeup artist at his studio so that these essential pieces can be built.

Have you ever watched a movie and noticed family photos in the background? Or perhaps you've seen a family picture sitting on an executive's office desk? These photos need to be taken prior to filming, so it is possible you will have a photo shoot that will allow the *art department* to put these props together.

On most TV shows and movies, the actors partake in a table read. Essentially, this is the first time the entire cast sits around a table reading the script out loud. This is led by the director while the writers, producers, and studio and/or network executives watch. In episodic television, the script is constantly changing up until the day of the shoot, so after a table read the production staff will meet to discuss their notes.

On feature films, if enough time has been allotted, the director might run rehearsals with his cast. This process allows him to work scenes out before the cameras roll, essentially saving time once shooting begins. It's also beneficial to the actors as it gives them a chance to bond. Rehearsals can take place on the actual set or location, or in a separate rehearsal space. Compensation for rehearsals, like any other preproduction activity involving the actor, is negotiated into an actor's contract.

The Night Before

Clients often get nervous and start calling me in the afternoon asking if I've heard anything about their call time for the next day. When you are booked on a film or TV show, you most likely will not hear from anyone about your call time until the night before your first day of work. Call times cannot be assigned until production is wrapped for the day because the unions require ample **turnaround time** before actors can report back to set. So once shooting has wrapped, one of the assistant directors (ADs) will call you with your call time for the following day.

You'll also be e-mailed a **call sheet** and a map. A call sheet gives you all of the pertinent information you need to know for the following shoot day. It includes your call time, the shooting location, and the scenes that will be shot. It also lists all pertinent phone numbers in case of emergency or if you get lost on the way to set.

A map is provided to help you find your way to the location. Sometimes, because of limited space near the actual location, parking will be in one spot while the physical set is farther away. In those instances, production generally provides a shuttle to take you from the parking lot to the set. Try to arrive a little bit early, or, at the very least, be punctual. Being late doesn't make a great impression and doesn't move people to hire you back again. So be sure you leave enough time for traffic.

Once You Arrive

As soon as you arrive on set, check in with the AD. She, in turn, will notify everyone of your arrival and that you're ready for whatever they need you to do. She might tell you to go hang out, in which case you can relax in your dressing room and practice your lines. She might send you off to hair and makeup right away. She might ask you to get into the wardrobe that is hanging in your trailer. Whatever the case may be, hop to it.

The truth is, there's a lot of downtime on set. You'll find yourself sitting around just waiting until they are ready for you. Filming can be exciting, but for those of us who have spent a lot of time on set, it can also be quite boring while you're waiting for your next scene. Bring some things to occupy your time: a portable DVD player, games, books, study material, etc. You're more than welcome to watch them shoot other scenes—just don't get in the way. And don't wander off too far, because when they do finally call you, they'll want you right away.

Paperwork

As I indicated earlier, on larger roles in bigger projects, the contract will be signed before you ever get to set. But if you're only working a few days on a movie, or you're working in episodic television, chances are you will be handed a contract to sign soon after you arrive on set. Unless you are familiar with contracts and know what to look for, don't sign anything.

I always advise my clients to call me or their agent once they have a contract in hand. That way, they can read it to us over the phone so we can make sure that it is correct. Often, clients will arrive on set very early and well before I make it to the office. They all know they can call my cell phone for something this important.

And what do I look for in these contracts? Basically, I want to make sure that the contract reflects the deal we negotiated. It's not that I believe anyone is trying to get away with any monkey business, but sometimes mistakes are made and, in my role as my client's protector, it's just smart to make sure the contract is correct before an actor signs anything.

Specifically, I look for the same things we negotiated up front in the *deal memo*. The pay rate tells me what the actor's salary shall be. The guarantee tells me how many days the actor was promised on this project. And billing tells me where his credit will be placed in the finished product. Those are the basics, but some additional issues may arise.

Until I am satisfied with the contract, I tell my actor not to sign. Ninety-nine percent of the time, there are no problems. But every once in a while, a problem may come up. In that case, I get on the phone with the AD and resolve the issue, generally quite quickly, as shooting can't commence until the contract is signed.

On the Clock

Even though you sign in when you get to set (and sign out when you leave), it's a smart idea to keep track of your own hours as well. You can jot them in a notebook, enter them into your laptop, or even log them in your journal that you started earlier (see page 72). This way, if any questions pop up after you've wrapped, you have a record of how long you worked.

Because actors are protected by their unions, you can only work a certain amount of hours without the production incurring financial penalties. Typically, on shoots involving children, a production won't work kids longer than the union allows because doing so would be a violation of labor laws, which could result in financial penalties. But if you are of legal age, you will be able to work overtime and earn extra money. You will be paid time and a half after a certain number of hours and double time on holidays. If you do not receive your meal break before six hours after your call time, you will also receive a *meal penalty*. And if you don't have at least twelve hours of rest from when you wrap until your call time the next day, you will receive a penalty payment for that as well. If you ever have a question, check with your union for more details.

These rules are designed with safety in mind so that actors are not overworked. As you'll see in chapter 10, additional hours are set aside for children to get their education on set while they are working.

Food, Glorious Food

One of the highlights of working on set is that there's always lots of food around. Meals are catered, and when it's not mealtime, craft services stocks a healthy supply of snacks. If you are working for the length of the project and have any special dietary needs, you might want to let production know. Set caterers are used to dealing with all sorts of different diets (from vegan and vegetarian to low-fat and low-carb) and are generally prepared to make everyone happy. If you're like me, and can't help snacking when there's food in front of you, stay far away from the craft services area!

Trailers

As we discussed on page 134, trailers and dressing rooms are pre-negotiated. The largest trailer is called a star wagon. It's full sized and is designated for one person. This is what movie stars receive, so don't feel bad if you don't get this perk for a while. Typically, a single trailer can hold multiple actors as it is divided into private rooms. One-half of a double banger means there are two rooms, one for each actor. One-third of a triple banger means there are three rooms, one for each actor. The smallest trailer is called a honey wagon. Most trailers come with a private bathroom, refrigerator, couch, and TV. Some come equipped with a stereo and DVD player as well. Honey wagons, however, tend to be barebones.

When children are on set, a trailer or study area, separate from the child's trailer, is set aside for schoolwork. That way, the child can work with the set teacher while Mom reads her book back at the trailer.

■ ■ ■

We'll examine the role of the teacher on set in chapter 10 and discuss a parent's role on set in chapter 11. But first, now that you've got your first job under your belt, it's time to tell everyone about it. Creating buzz and generating interest in you as an actor is integral to furthering your career. And now that we've got something to talk about, the job becomes just a little easier.

THE POWER OF PUBLICITY

Publicist Ron Scott signed a young John Stamos when he was first cast as Blackie Parrish on *General Hospital*. "I had never represented an actor who hit so fast," recalls Scott.

Stamos was brought onto the ABC soap for what was supposed to be a short-term gig. But Scott hit the publicity immediately. "I set up interviews and photo shoots with *Tiger Beat, 16, Teen Beat,* and *Super Teen* magazines right away," says Scott. "At the end of each article we requested the fans write to John in care of ABC. The minute the issues hit the stands, thousands of fans were writing to John. I remember visiting him in his dressing room and there were mail bags literally stacked to the ceiling, full of letters from adoring fans."

Needless to say, the producers offered Stamos a three-year contract and gave him a huge increase in salary. And he has been going strong ever since. From *Full House* to *ER*, he has worked consistently throughout the years and remains one of the busiest actors in Hollywood today.

■ ■ ■

A job is great, but if no one knows about it, in Hollywood, that's like it never happened. This chapter discusses how to maximize publicity opportunities connected to any job you do. We'll also discuss how to create buzz within the industry and help propel your career to the next level.

Your Own Best Agent

You have to be your own best agent. It's an ancient Hollywood proverb that you've probably heard before. But what does it mean? And does it apply to actors who already have representation or just to those who are starting out without an agent at all?

It applies to everybody. In fact, I even tell it to my own clients, whom I work very hard for. But no matter how intensely your team works for you, and no matter how good they may be, no one can sell you better than you can. It's just a fact of life.

I can pick up the phone, call everyone I know in Tinseltown and talk you up until I'm blue in the face. But that's nothing compared to your meeting with someone personally and getting them excited in the room. Charming industry players goes back to the threshold skills that I discussed earlier in chapter 6.

Being your own best agent also involves beating down every door you can and never taking no for an answer. "Try to do something every day that will help your career," says Melissa Berger, an agent with CESD. "Set goals: long-term and intermediate goals that are accessible and realistic. You need to find things that will make you feel good about yourself that will bring you toward your goals. There's so much potential for failure in this business, you need to set up things that you win along the way."

"Always be helpful and nice on set, because they'll want to use you again," advises agent Judy Savage. "Keep up your skills. Even if you only have one line in a movie, make sure it's the best one line that could have been done—they may write in more lines for you. Perseverance always pays off. If you know in your heart and soul that this is the only thing you want to do in life, keep studying and don't give up."

Creating Buzz

Creating buzz is what I do for a living. In a way, my goal is to conjure up so much excitement about an actor that everyone wants to meet him. But that's not always easy to accomplish, so sometimes I have to get a little creative.

It's one thing to make a call and say that my client just starred opposite Johnny Depp in the biggest movie of the year. But most of my clients haven't achieved that level of stardom yet. In fact, some are developmental and just starting out.

With someone who is brand new, I still need to create buzz, so I talk about why he was so exciting to me when I first met him.

Was it a physical feature? Did something amazing happen the first time I saw him read? Was he the most sought-after actor at IMTA (International Model & Talent Association)? Does he have a smile that can melt your heart? Whatever it happens to be, I share my proud discovery and make the person to whom I'm speaking feel like he's discovering this actor for the first time as well.

With a client who is not brand new, but maybe hasn't booked a whole lot yet, I focus on all the progress she's made thus far. She gets callbacks on almost everything she's been in on. She's been on avail a number of times. Casting director Leslie Zaslower told me that she's a brilliant actor who she'll continue to bring back in the future for any role she might fit.

Obviously, the more an actor has booked, the easier it is to generate excitement. Sabrina just booked an episode of *The Unit*. Did you happen to catch Annamarie on *Medium* last night? Did you know that Andy tested for eight pilots in the last two years?

Your challenge is to take what I do on behalf of my clients and do it for yourself. You've got to create and disperse your own buzz. Analyze where you are in your career, and come up with a great sales pitch. But be careful—it's one thing for me to tell people how wonderful you are, but it might come off as cocky or arrogant when you do it yourself. So be extra thoughtful when discussing your accomplishments.

Show confidence, but also humility. Talk about the positive experiences you've had since you've been in L.A., while you've been auditioning and when you've worked on other shows or films. When you're out and about meeting new people in the industry and networking with those who could potentially help you, it's not the time to be shy. However, when you're with other actors, you might not want to rub your successes in their faces. There's a right time and a wrong time to self-promote, so carefully navigate each situation, and once you're convinced the person is interested in knowing more about you, do your thing and make him or her a fan.

Moms and dads need to find the line between assertively promoting their children and being annoying stage parents. It's fine to network on behalf of your child, but the same rules apply. There is always a right time and place for this, so make sure your actions are appropriate.

Fans

The other group of people you need to sell yourself to is your fans. I'm not talking about people in the industry who become fans. I mean real, legitimate, autograph-seeking, picture-snapping fans. While fans might factor in a little later in your career, it's amazing how quickly you can blow up once you start working—especially in children's television. One of my clients worked on *Hannah Montana*. The moment his episodes began to air, he could barely leave his house without being recognized.

Treat your fans well and with the utmost respect. These are the people who will watch your next show, see your next film, and buy your next CD. Be good to them and they will be fans for life. A few years ago, I went to a concert that my friend Joey McIntyre gave. When he was a kid, Joe was a member of the pop group New Kids on the Block. Would you believe, his concert was packed with women in their thirties and forties that had been fans since they were kids? I've got to give Joe credit, because that kind of loyalty only comes from maintaining a positive relationship with your fans.

Be mindful of how you handle yourself in public. Young actors and actors who have young fans are constantly under the microscope and in the public eye. Your fans want to be just like you. So if they see you smoking, or acting rude, or drinking before you're twenty-one, what kind of message will that send to them? You might not have asked for it, but being an actor comes with a certain amount of responsibility. You need to be a good role model. If you start acting irresponsibly, you might find yourself not only losing fans but also losing jobs because of your volatile reputation.

"Stay focused, and make sure you really love acting and your profession . . . because if you don't, the millions of distractions and temptations will get the best of you," warns Michelle Lewitt of the Casting Company. "Never believe your own hype, because sooner or later other people won't. Hard work is always rewarded in the long run. Keep a big-picture mentality, and if you start to love the fame more than the work, get out of the biz."

"Always handle yourself in a professional manner," adds manager Jamie Malone. "This town is a big town, but a small town. Bad behavior is *toxic*. You never know who you're in the presence of."

If you're one of the lucky ones who becomes a star, you'll probably need to look into fan club services. Yes, there are actually companies that you can hire to handle and respond to all of your fan mail. While you're still on your way to that place, this can be a great job for Mom and Dad.

Official Website

One great way to communicate with your fans and keep people abreast of your career is to create an official website. Prices to set up and maintain a professional website vary, but in this competitive market you can shop around for a good deal. Even before you have anything to publicize, you should purchase your name as your domain name (e.g., www.fredericklevy.com) before it gets snatched up.

A website can service your acting business in so many positive ways. It can update users about your upcoming projects. You can share exclusive photos and video content with fans online. An official site can allow fans to interact with you through e-mail, as well as interact with each other through message boards. It can also help you collect contact information in a database so you can maintain a mailing list for sending out publicity blasts.

Start a MySpace and Facebook fan page. You can maintain a personal page as well. But again, be careful what you write and what pictures you post. If it's something that may not show you in the best light, remove it immediately.

In a world where technology is constantly advancing, and in a business that embraces this technology, I highly recommend getting on the information superhighway. But be careful. Don't publish any personal information that you want to keep private. While it's common to list your representations' contact information on your site, never list your own. Online material that is used to generate work like an electronic press kit or an online reel should be accessed separately through a private page that can be given exclusively to industry personnel through your handlers.

A NOTE ABOUT SAFETY

This is for parents, but really it's smart advice for anyone in the public eye. When you register for a website or any other service, you'll often be asked for your address. Never give this information out. Instead, purchase a post office box and use this as your mailing address.

Unfortunately, there are some crazy people in this world: stalkers, obsessed fans, etc. You read about them in the gossip rags all the time. So if you're planning for a career in the public eye, be smart and block your private information from public records to the best of your ability. Taking precautions like this is a necessary part of the business.

Spreading the Word

They say that all publicity is good publicity. I tend to believe it. I remember a client calling me in a panic because TMZ had printed a story about him on their website and it was generating some unflattering comments from various anonymous users. He wanted to know what we could do to get TMZ to take the story down so that these negative comments would end. I quickly pointed out that when people *aren't* talking about him, then we've got serious problems. The fact that people cared enough to post anything at all was a really great sign. Besides, he made the front page of TMZ—you can't buy that kind of publicity!

Of course, when a young actor's ego is involved, there can be a downside to negative press. I tell my clients and the parents of my younger child actors to ignore it to the best of their abilities. It can be hard to resist, especially in today's media-obsessed society, but just don't read the tabloids; don't even read the reviews of your work. And if you happen to read a negative comment, whether about your performance or appearance, remember not to take it personally; all it is, is one person's opinion of one thing you've done. You'll have many more chances throughout your career to prove the naysayers wrong or change their minds. Mom and Dad need to comfort and rebuild confidence in kids hurt by this negativity.

Publicity can be expensive. In a town where it costs between $3,000 and $4,000 a month to maintain a personal publicist, many actors, especially young actors, and especially young actors who are just starting out, simply cannot afford this expense. So you need to get creative in your approach to spreading the word about your career.

I put together my own press kits (hard copy and electronic) with the help of my clients. You can assemble one on your own as well. Any time there's a newspaper clipping or magazine article or great review, I ask my client to get me a copy—and it becomes part of our kit. We throw in a couple great still shots from film or TV appearances, a current headshot, and a biography that I write (see, there *is* an advantage to having a manager who is also a writer). I then mail or e-mail these kits out to prospective press requests as well as to casting and studio executives. A press kit can look quite professional and impressive if it's put together well. In fact, sending out a kit on a client has sometimes made the difference between getting him in a room and not getting that opportunity at all.

I also like to put together a publicity reel on my clients. This differs from an acting reel because, rather than showcasing a client's talent, it spotlights her exposure through clips of televised interviews she has done. This reel can be used to show news magazine shows like *Entertainment Tonight* and *Access Hollywood* how comfortable an actor can be when she is being interviewed on camera.

Another way you can publicize yourself is through mailings. Want to let everyone know you're guest starring on *Entourage*? Want to alert the casting community that you're opening in a new show at the Geffen? Would you like to announce that you've just been cast as a lead in the new Julia Roberts flick? These are all great opportunities to put your name and face in front of the people who hire actors.

"I always opt for self-promotion via mailings and e-mails when you are in something or have an airdate," says Bryan Leder of BLT Management. "Target the date and hit hard. If it's a live show, get as many industry comps [free tickets for industry professionals to come see your work] as you can, and have your reps send out invites. My client is going to Broadway early next year in a new musical that started its pre-Broadway run in L.A. It was amazing to see over forty casting professionals go to this show who were hoping to catch it anyway. Because we invited them, our client now has forty new relationships. The positive results are immeasurable."

Charity

Getting involved with various charities can have a positive effect on many levels. As your star rises, you can really do a lot of good by bringing attention to a particular cause that you believe in. And you will benefit as well. Most charities put on big fundraising events. To draw people into these events, they invite celebrities to attend. This of course garners publicity for both the actors who participate as well as the charity. And I can't imagine anything but good press coming from good deeds like this. But don't just throw yourself to a cause in order to be photographed. There are so many great charities out there—stand behind the ones that truly matter to you.

Of course, until your star rises, you may not rate a celebrity invite. That shouldn't stop you from getting involved with some of these groups. In addition to doing helpful work, you may also find yourself presented with great opportunities to meet likeminded individuals. And who knows? Maybe a meaningful friendship or even a viable networking opportunity will present itself.

■ ■ ■

The next two chapters are designed especially for kids in the business and their parents. If you've already turned eighteen and have a high school diploma, feel free to skip to chapter 12 to see how we put it all together and call it a wrap. Otherwise, turn the page to explore the industry as it relates to children and their parents.

FOR KIDS ONLY

Talent agent Vivian Hollander has been working with young actors for more than twenty years. In that time, she's seen just about everything, which is why she triple-checks every detail, including the validity of her young clients' **work permits**. One of her clients booked a commercial that was to work the Tuesday after Columbus Day. Hollander called her client's parents to verify that their daughter's work permit was valid, and they assured her it was.

On the Monday holiday, Hollander received an anxious phone call from her client's parents telling her that they had yet to receive the valid permit in the mail. "This was in spite of the fact that I had phoned last week to confirm that the work permit was in order. The parents had assured me it was," says an agitated Hollander.

Because it was a holiday and the labor office was closed, there was absolutely no way to obtain even an emergency permit in time to do the job. And, as expected, the job went bye-bye. Clearly, this is not the way Hollander likes to conduct her business. "They want the kids to bring their work permits to set," says Hollander. "No matter how many times you tell them, they confirm, but then they're caught in a lie. This time it cost them the job."

■　■　■

This chapter details the rules and regulations pertaining to kids in the business. While you don't need to be an expert, you should be familiar with child labor laws. I'll tell you how to get your child a work permit and set up a *Coogan account*. I'll also explore education options from home school to regular school to on-set education.

Child Labor Law

Believe it or not, children who are employed as actors or performers are exempt from the Fair Labor Standards Act (FLSA), which limits the number of hours a child can work and when that child can work. This is because child actors have their own set of laws that pertain to their work in the entertainment business. While the laws differ from state to state, those that govern Los Angeles and New York City are very similar. I will cover these rules in this chapter. If your child is hired as an actor in a state other than California or New York, you should refer to your state's Department of Labor for rules specific to your area.

For children who were hired in Los Angeles or New York City but are working outside of California and New York, know that the laws that govern child actors in the state where they were hired are strictly enforced in the new location. This holds true if your child should shoot a film or television show out of the country as well.

Entertainment Work Permits

Minors aged fifteen days to eighteen years employed in the entertainment and recording industries must have a work permit issued by the Department of Labor. These permits are also required for minors in California who are employed as models in the fashion industry. Permits are required even when the project is noncommercial in nature.

There is no fee to get a work permit. You must simply fill out an application completely and mail it, along with any required documents and a pre-addressed, stamped envelope, to any office of the Division of Labor Standards Enforcement. A permit may also be filed in person.

WORK PERMIT APPLICATIONS

To download a work permit application, visit the following websites:

California: www.dir.ca.gov/dlse/DLSEForm277.pdf

New York: www.labor.state.ny.us/formsdocs/wp/LS561.pdf

Work permits are valid for up to six months, but be sure to renew your child's permit thirty days prior to expiration. You don't want to be caught without a valid permit when your child books a role. As we saw in the case of Vivian Hollander's client, not having a valid permit could cost your child the job. Likewise, make sure you bring that work permit to set, as the production will require seeing it.

In addition to the application, you will need to submit additional documentation to get a work permit. Most states require a letter from your child's school stating that she is in good academic standing. You will also need a copy of your child's birth certificate. Finally, in California and New York, you will also need to provide proof of a blocked trust account, sometimes known as a Coogan account, discussed on the next page.

PASSPORTS

In addition to having a valid work permit, it's also a good idea to have a valid passport. So many jobs film internationally, and you never know when you might need to travel outside the country for work. And parents, your child isn't the only one who needs a valid passport—you will need one, too, since you will most likely be traveling with him. "I represent a set of twins who were trying really hard and working really hard, but they hadn't booked anything yet," recalls agent Melissa Berger. "They finally booked a commercial that would take them out of the country, but they couldn't do it because the passports weren't there."

Sometimes a child books a job and the parent doesn't realize the permit had expired. Depending on when the role works, there may be enough time to renew the work permit through regular methods—it generally takes up to several weeks for the Department of Labor to process an application once they receive it. In these rare circumstances, we have been able to get a letter from the production stating that the child was hired and would be working within the next few days. The parents took this letter, and all the other required documents, to the labor office. The office, in turn, expedited the permit process and issued an immediate work permit while the parents waited. But this is an exception to the rule. Always allow plenty of time to get your permit renewed. You do not want to rely on getting an expedited permit every time, because expedition is not guaranteed.

Coogan Accounts

Coogan accounts are "blocked trust" accounts that are created to set aside 15 percent of a child's earnings for him until he turns eighteen. These accounts are required by California, New York, Louisiana, and New Mexico, and, in most cases, you will have to show proof of an account to get your work permit.

The Coogan Law is named after child actor Jackie Coogan who, after a successful acting career in his youth, found that he had nothing left by the time he turned twenty-one. He had to sue his mother for his money, and this led to the creation of the Coogan Law, to protect this type of crime from happening again. While Coogan was able to recover a small portion of his earnings, he later went on to find success as an adult actor, most notably in the role of Uncle Fester on *The Addams Family* TV show.

In California, a Coogan account must be opened with a California bank. Most banks, credit unions, and brokerage firms offer blocked trust accounts. However, not all banking institutions provide this service, and even those that do still have employees who are unfamiliar with this type of account.

In New York, Louisiana, and New Mexico, the blind trust isn't called a Coogan account. You must ask to open a UTMA- (Uniform Transfer to Minors Act) or UGMA- (Uniform Gift to Minors Act) compliant trust account. Also, unlike in California where you must open a Coogan account in a California bank, the UTMA account required by New York labor law can be opened in any bank, in any state. In addition, should the balance in the account reach $250,000, a trust company must be appointed as custodian of the account.

In all cases, if you wish to put more than 15 percent into the child's trust account, you may. But remember, after taxes, commissions, and the automatic 15 percent deduction, there may not be a lot of money left over from your child's paycheck. Be smart and invest some of your child's earnings back into your child's career on headshots, classes, and other business expenses.

Education

Education must be a top priority for any children who want to work in the entertainment industry. The biggest reason is because without maintaining a satisfactory academic performance, a child cannot get a work permit. And since you must submit a letter from your school every time you renew your permit, you must always have good grades.

"Keeping grades up so you can get a work permit goes without saying—it's like breathing," says Melissa Berger, an agent with CESD. "Otherwise, it's six months that you're out of the game [or until you receive your next report card]. If you really want to be in this business, you have to make fulfilling your scholastic obligations equally as important as your artistic goals."

Be practical. Education is important, period. If you want to get ahead in life, no matter what it is you end up doing, a solid education lays the foundation for most of your future opportunities.

On set, education continues to be a priority in a young actor's day. If a child is guaranteed three or more consecutive days of employment, then a studio teacher will be provided on set. In addition, if a minor is employed but is not entitled to have a teacher, that child shall be taught by the studio teacher who is instructing another child on set if the first child's regular school is in session. A single studio teacher may not teach more than ten children, unless those children are in second grade or below, in which case she may teach twenty children.

Producers are required to have a school facility, separate from the actor's trailer, where the child is taught. They also provide whatever teaching equipment and school supplies are necessary. However, it is the parent's responsibility to get school assignments and bring textbooks from the school the actor normally attends, for use on set. This will allow the set teacher to help the young actors stay on top of their regular curriculum.

SCHOOL TIES

Children in the entertainment industry have a variety of schooling options at their disposal when they are not working. Some are enrolled in regular public and private schools like most kids throughout the country. Others are homeschooled by their parents. Still others are enrolled in distance learning programs, which are gaining popularity quickly.

Distance learning programs differ from homeschooling in that most are offered by accredited private schools. The way they work is as follows: Withdraw your child from her current school and enroll her in one of these schools at the same level at which she is currently studying. If you move back to your hometown for any reason, just withdraw your child from the distance learning school, request her transcripts, and then enroll her back into the school she left.

The following is a list of public and private homeschool and distance learning programs:

Abbington Hill School: www.school-your-way.com
The California Virtual Academies: www.k12.com/cava
Excellence in Education: www.excellenceineducation.com
Internet Home School: www.internethomeschool.com
K12: www.k12.com
Laurel Springs Home School: www.laurelsprings.com
Options for Youth: www.ofy.org

The set teacher determines the required number of hours for instruction each day, keeping in mind that a child must be taught an average of at least three hours per day. The maximum amount of school time in any one day varies by grade. For kindergarten, it's four hours; for grades 1–6, five hours; and for grades 7–12, six hours. Sometimes on set when things are taking longer to set up, the child will be sent to do schoolwork and be brought back when the cameras are ready to roll. However, no period of less than twenty minutes is counted as school time. So if producers send you to the schoolroom, they must know they won't need you for at least twenty minutes.

Just because a teacher is on set doesn't mean that parents no longer have to be responsible for their children. A parent or guardian must be present at all times while a child is working. These adults have the right, subject to filming requirements, to be within sight and sound of their child at all times. However, this rule does not extend to the classroom.

TEACHER TEACHER

The primary role of a studio teacher on set is to ensure that the child labor laws are followed any time a minor works within the entertainment industry. Essentially, this means providing for the education, safety, health, and welfare of child actors. "While the kids are filming, I'm working with production to make sure they are as safe and comfortable as possible while only working the hours allowed by California's labor laws," explains Scott Plimpton, a studio teacher who has worked on such shows as *Unfabulous, All That,* and *Just Jordan*.

Plimpton's interactions on set focus on three separate categories: production, parents, and the minors themselves.

"Enforcing the law on production is probably my least favorite role but a vital one," says Plimpton. "There is often a significant amount of pressure on set to 'get the shot,' and even the best intentioned production crew can become caught up in the moment and lose sight of what is legally possible. Most commonly this means asking a minor only allowed to work a certain number of hours (it varies by age group) to work ten, twenty, thirty minutes or more past their legal limits. If that time is the difference between a child actor being involved in a scene or being cut from it, is a parent going to say no? Usually not."

It's up to the teacher to remind production that what they're asking for just isn't possible. Plimpton tries to come up with a solution that will satisfy production but keep the plan within the legal limits. "It might mean breaking the scene apart and only shooting the minor's part for the last hour and then once the minor is wrapped, going back to shoot the adult's part," says Plimpton. "There is almost always a solution. It's just a matter of being creative and finding it."

Plimpton believes the biggest contribution he makes to parents is giving them the confidence that while their child is on set, every reasonable precaution will be taken to safeguard that child's well-being. "If a scene calls for a minor actor to run across an outdoor field barefoot I'll remind production to sweep that field for sharp stones, glass, thorns, etc. before they shoot it," says Plimpton. "If a face full of salsa is called for (yes, it's happened more than once!), I'll check with props to make sure they are not using real salsa with all of the eye-irritating onions and peppers it contains but a mild look-alike alternative. Oftentimes production and props have already thought of these things, but not always. My difference is to make sure it is always [thought of]."

Plimpton also strives to make certain that each day minor actors have school on set, they will leave the set better informed about the world and the subjects they are studying. "It doesn't happen every time, but if at the end of the day a minor is talking to his parents about why the Greeks didn't invent algebra instead of who he met or what he did that day, well, then I especially feel like I made a difference," admits Plimpton.

As for the minors themselves, Plimpton tries to earn their trust and spark a passion for all that the world has to offer. "Minor actors are in a unique position to influence our national, and even on occasion, global culture," explains Plimpton. "If I am able to instill the values of curiosity, education, and knowledge within them, I know that will make a difference."

One of Plimpton's happiest moments came when a child actor actually went to a nearby bookstore during their lunch break to purchase several books from a series they both enjoyed and donated them to his traveling library. "He wanted to make sure other students could enjoy them," reveals Plimpton.

Teacher of the Year Plimpton has a keen desire to try for himself anything a minor is asked to do. "The firsthand experience of doing what is being requested of the actor is very beneficial to me in judging the safety and appropriateness of that action," says Plimpton. "Bottom line: I'm not comfortable asking a minor to do something I wouldn't be willing to do myself."

This philosophy has led to some very interesting experiences on set. "I've eaten a worm (a little chewy but actually rather bland), cradled a possum (turns out their tails go right for your belt loops and are rather hard to remove!), flipped backwards off a swing (easier than it sounds and looks), and had a variety of props bounced off my head (it's amazing how realistic Nerf material can look on film)," says Plimpton.

By far Plimpton's favorite experience occurred while working with Devon Werkheiser on a promotion for the SpongeBob special *Atlantis SquarePantis*. "We were flown down to a resort in the Bahamas where Devon was going to film an underwater interview in a huge aquarium at the resort," says Plimpton. "To do this he had to be comfortable wearing specialized diving equipment that allowed him to talk underwater. Obviously a test run of the equipment was necessary, and production was kind enough to allow me to be part of it."

The only area available for the test was the shark tank! For about thirty minutes or so, Devon, Scott, and a member of the production team got geared up and went for a walk with the sharks. Like most exciting entertainment, this sounds much more dangerous than it actually was. "Besides being of the typically harmless variety, these sharks were also the fattest, best fed sharks I have ever seen," admits Plimpton. "They could barely rouse themselves to get out of our way, much less show any interest in what we tasted like. Devon even reached out and touched the tail of one that just couldn't be bothered to move!"

The experience was not only a highlight of the trip for Plimpton, but it also provided him with valuable information when overseeing the actual filming. "I knew just how heavy the helmet was and that outside of the water it was extremely awkward and destabilizing to have it resting on your shoulders," explains Plimpton. "This meant that one of the most critical times for supervision would be when Devon had to climb in and out of the water when the weight of the helmet wasn't supported by water. I was also reminded that the rungs of the ladder underwater were the most slippery. Not that I actually slipped or anything. I simply realized how easy and understandable it would be for something like that to happen."

The shoot went off without a hitch, and both Scott and Devon came home with all of their fingers and toes intact. If this doesn't make Plimpton teacher of the year, I'm not sure what else he can do!

The Hours

Labor laws dictate how long a minor is allowed to work each day. Work hours are determined by age. An infant who is fifteen days to six months old is only allowed to work twenty minutes per day and may only be at the employment site for a maximum of two hours. A studio teacher and nurse are required if the production is employing an infant. An infant may only work between the hours of 9:30 A.M. and 11:30 A.M. or 2:30 P.M. and 4:30 P.M.

Children who are between six months and two years old may work a maximum of two hours a day, and they're only allowed to be at the employment site for four hours. The other two hours must be used strictly for rest and recreation. These children can only work between the hours of 5 A.M. and 12:30 A.M. A parent or guardian must be present.

Children who are between the ages of two and six years old can work three hours a day, and they're only allowed to be at the employment site for six hours maximum. A studio teacher is required on set even during weekends, holidays, and school breaks. These children also can only work between the hours of 5 A.M. and 12:30 A.M.

When school is in session, minors who are between the ages of six and nine can work four hours a day, go to school for three hours, and have one hour of rest and recreation. They can only be at the employment site for a maximum of eight hours. When school is not in session, they can work for six hours a day. These children can only be employed between the hours of 5 A.M. and 12:30 A.M. except on school nights, when they can only work until 10 P.M.

When school is in session, minors who are between the ages of nine and sixteen can work five hours a day, must attend school three hours a day, and have one hour for rest and recreation. They may spend a total of nine hours daily at the site of employment. When school is out, they can work for seven hours with one hour for rest and recreation. Employment times are the same as above.

When school is in session, teens that are between the ages of sixteen and eighteen can work six hours a day, must attend school for three hours a day, and have one hour for rest and recreation. They may stay at the employment site for no more than ten hours. When school is not in session, they can work for eight hours a day with an additional hour for rest and recreation. Studio teachers are required for schooling. Employment times remain the same.

As you can see, from the production's perspective, it is more beneficial to hire an older actor who plays someone younger simply because older actors can work longer hours. This is true with kids who play younger than they truly are, and it's equally true for adults who can play kids and teens. Why hire a fifteen-year-old who can only work five hours a day when you can hire a twenty-year-old who looks fifteen and who can work a full day plus overtime if needed?

To protect themselves from losing jobs, some older teens take their high school equivalency exam, or GED, so that they can work the same number of hours as an adult. This can be quite attractive to prospective employers. However, doing this is a personal decision that each family must make at the right time.

"Education has always been a priority for me," says Vivian Hollander. "Equivalency tests are fine for kids who are being discriminated against because of their age. However, it is a very serious step to take and should be given a great deal of thought."

Hollander represented a young teen named Troy Slaten who she had put on the series *Parker Lewis Can't Lose*. He happened to be the only minor on the series, as all of the other cast members were over eighteen. After the first season the producers approached Hollander to ask if Slaten would be willing get his high school equivalency degree. "They said, 'We'd like to broaden his part, but it's difficult because he can only shoot so many hours,'" recalls Hollander. "We presented it to the parents and gave them all the pros and cons. His parents agreed as long as he could remain in school and make up work, with a tutor they provided, on the down times."

Everyone was happy. Slaten continued to work as an actor for several years until he decided he wanted to go to law school. Today he works as a criminal law and litigation attorney.

There are a few other rules you should be aware of. No minor can be employed over eight hours per day or over forty-eight hours in a week. Meal periods are not counted as work time. Generally, meals must be given within six hours of the call time and/or the previous meal, although studio teachers may demand earlier mealtimes. Workdays can extend up to one half hour for meals.

Travel between studio and location is considered work time. Twelve hours must elapse between wrap time and the next day's call time. Makeup applied in a child's home by a makeup artist employed by the production is also considered work time.

■ ■ ■

Don't worry if you can't remember all the rules. If there's ever a problem or a question, you can always call your agent, manager, or union representative. And when it comes to children's safety and security, there's no such thing as a silly question, so don't ever be afraid to speak up.

MOM-AGERS, POP-AGENTS,
AND THE VITAL ROLE OF PARENTS IN THE BIZ

Tina Mouser's best friend moved from Arkansas to Pennsylvania. During the summer following the move, Mouser went to visit her in Philadelphia. Little did she know, this trip to see her friend would change her family's lives.

Prior to their visit, Mouser's friend told her that her little boy had auditioned for a Disney World commercial and booked it. She also told her that a movie was going to be filmed in town and that the production was looking for a five-year-old girl. Tina's daughter Mary was five at the time. "She told me to take some pictures of Mary and send them to her," recalls Mouser. "Those were our headshots, since we didn't know what a headshot was."

When they arrived in Philadelphia, Mouser took her daughter to the casting office. "I gave them pictures that I had, but the assistant said, 'You're just here for a week—you probably won't get an audition,'" says Mouser. But just then, the casting director came out of his office and Mouser recognized him from his picture on the wall. She said hello. The casting director took an interest in this family from Arkansas and engaged Mouser in conversation. Even if they didn't get an audition, at least they got to meet the casting director, she reasoned.

The Mousers left the office soon thereafter. "Before we pulled out of the driveway, the casting director called to set auditions with all three of my kids for the movie *Signs*." Apparently they had made a good impression in the lobby.

The Mouser family went to the audition the next day and it was like a cattle call, with so many people there. "I figured that's what it was like," recalls Mouser. "If your child walks out with a piece of paper, it means they have a callback." Only two girls in that whole room got callbacks. Mary was one of them.

They went back for the callback the next day, but they didn't hear anything before it was time to leave town and return home. Months went by and they never heard from the casting office. They had nearly forgotten about the whole experience when they got a call checking on Mary's availability for *Signs*. They ultimately hired Mary as the photo double for future Oscar nominee Abigail Breslin.

Mary flourished on set, really enjoying the environment. And while she was only the photo double, everyone could tell she had a bright future in this business. "Kim Breslin [Abigail's mom] told me, 'Don't you ever, ever let that child do background again. She doesn't need to do background; she needs to be doing this herself,'" recalls Mouser. "It was a way for us to get into a business that we never thought about in our wildest dreams. It changed our lives, but it was meant to be."

I Can Do That

When I'm scouting for talent, I'll often meet parents who tell me that they are their child's manager. I don't care how great the kid might be, I run. Sure, before your child has professional representation, maybe you feel like you're managing her career, so why not take the credit?

Let me state right off the bat that I don't approve of mom-agers and pop-agents—parents who think they can be their own child's representation. I think it's a horrible idea that defeats the whole purpose of having representation in the first place.

Are Mom and Dad really going to pick up the phone and chat with casting directors about their child's career? Do they even have the necessary relationships to make those calls? And even if they do, how will anyone take them seriously when they're pitching their own kid?

Can they be objective when a casting director gives them negative feedback on their child's audition? Can they still demand respect at home while they're working for their teenagers? Are they really setting their child up for success by preventing them from signing with a manager who has more experience?

I'm not saying that in the history of the entertainment business there hasn't ever been a successful agent or manager who got into the business because his or her child was a kid actor. But I have also seen families fall apart as a result of parents representing their own children. It's a horrible thing to witness and presumably worse to go through.

"The best thing parents can do for their children who are involved in the entertainment industry is provide moral and emotional support," suggests Julie Fulop, a youth agent with AKA. "Managing talent is not the same as being a parent. Being a manager is a full-time job that should be left to those who are professionally adept at doing that job and have done so for many years.

"In an industry that is as difficult and competitive as ours, it is so very crucial that parents provide the support system their child needs," Fulop continues. "With the moral and emotional support of his parents, the child can only benefit and be able to make the transition far more smoothly from youth actor to adult actor."

"Make sure that you get a good manager and agent—people who truly believe in your child as much as you do," advises Mouser. "The biggest drawback for me is that I get too involved in what other people say. I listen to things that I shouldn't. So stay focused on your child and what her goals are, and let the professionals do their jobs."

Leave the coaching to the professionals. Unless you too are an actor or have had formal acting training, please don't coach your kids on how to deliver their lines. If your kids are too young to read, say the lines to them as neutrally as possible and let their own instincts guide them in delivering those lines. If your kids are older and they just need someone to read with so they can practice, focus on being a good reader. Sometimes even the most well-intentioned direction can throw them off, so try to refrain from offering your advice on how they should act. "This can be tricky, as some parents are innately better at this than others," says acting coach Dennis LaValle. "Worse, some think they are great at it and only wind up messing it up for the child."

"If the child can read, help him to become very familiar with the material and then get him coached," Lavalle advises. "If the child can't read yet, explain the sides to him as if you were telling him a story and then read him the material, playing all the parts to the best of your ability. In addition, read all the stage directions so he can get a sense of what is going on. Then most definitely get him coached. Be careful not to have him memorize the material before a coaching, as his performance will almost always be hopelessly locked."

Parents do have a very important role in their child's career—as parents. Let the professionals do what they do best so you can focus on your vital position. You're an extremely important part of the team as we navigate your child's career in the entertainment industry.

What You Should Be Doing

Now that we've established what you shouldn't be doing, let's discuss what your role should be. In the beginning, when you're just starting out and thinking about a show business career for your child, you are a researcher. You're reading books like this one to educate yourself about what it takes to launch a child actor. You're surfing the Web for resources that will help guide you on this adventure and answer some of your questions. You're looking into acting classes, talent conventions, and perhaps an exploratory trip to Los Angeles to see the lay of the land.

"When my daughter Allie was six years old and just getting interested in this, I was still very uneducated about how the business works," reveals Angie Grant. "She had gotten several callbacks at a talent convention. I thought that she could sign with all of them."

That was not the case, and Grant soon got a harsh dose of reality. "A manager said to me, 'The best thing you can do is go back to Mississippi and learn about the business and then come back, because you have a very special child,'" recalls Grant. And that's exactly what she did.

Grant returned to Mississippi and started doing her homework. "I found an acting coach in Nashville, Tennessee," she recalls. "Every week, we'd make an eight-hour round trip, for a one-hour acting lesson. But it's a different playground out here [in L.A.]. You want your child at the best level possible so they can compete with the kids who are out here." Grant also enrolled her daughter with a speech pathologist to help her get rid of her strong Southern accent.

Finally, Grant decided to make a few exploratory trips to Los Angeles to make sure this was the right thing to do before uprooting her family and moving to L.A. for good. "Don't just move here permanently," cautions Grant. "Come during pilot season or episodics. Don't just pick up and move. Test the waters first."

This strategy seemed to work very well for the Grants. Two weeks after their third visit to L.A., Allie booked a series regular role on *Weeds* as Elizabeth Perkins's daughter, Isabel.

You're also the chauffeur, certainly if your kids are too young to drive themselves. Your job is to map out directions to each audition and shuttle your child to and fro. Think of each audition as a job interview. You wouldn't be late for such an appointment, so be sure to get little Shaina there on time as well. And if you're frustrated by the traffic, try and keep it to yourself. Don't put added pressure on your kids, who should be using the time in the car to focus on doing a great job in the room.

When you are in the waiting room of the casting office, keep everything close to the vest. In other words, this is not your time to socialize with the other stage moms. Nobody there is your friend. "It's really simple," says Bryan Leder. "Ask yourself this question: 'Do they really want my child to book a job over theirs?'"

While you are waiting, it's okay to eavesdrop. You may find out some valuable information about another audition your child is right for. Give this "scoop" to your agent so he can vet it and, if appropriate, get an appointment. But don't be the one giving out this valuable insight. If your kid has other auditions set up, don't start sharing this with his competition. Let the competition figure that out on their own. "There is absolutely no positive reason for moms to be exchanging information," says agent Vivian Hollander. "Information is often incorrect and tends to inflame and not help in any way."

Fulop agrees: "Every child is different. Every job is different. Moms who exchange information about their children's auditions in the waiting room should be avoided. Sometimes it is incorrect information that doesn't benefit anyone. There are so many factors as to why talent is seen and whom casting chooses to bring into their sessions. Details go far beyond what age is listed on the breakdown."

One time Mary Mouser had both a movie audition and a commercial audition in the same afternoon. They went to the movie audition first and it went very well. Later, at the commercial audition, a mother recognized Mary and told mom Tina that her kid had already received a callback for the movie they had just auditioned for.

"Mary's face dropped—she was clearly disappointed," recalls the elder Mouser. "Needless to say, she didn't book the commercial, either. We've learned to not pay attention to lobby chatter, to stay away from it, and not let other people affect us."

And while I'll repeat that I'm strongly against mom-agers, it is part of your job to monitor the representation and make sure they're working hard and doing a great job for your child. That doesn't mean you have to hound them every five minutes to ask for another audition. You will know if they're doing good work by their communication style with you and the rest of the team, and by your child's level of activity.

One of the most important roles of a parent is that of comforter. Actors in general need a lot of moral support in this business. It's not easy. Believe it or not, some kids deal with rejection better than adults. But not all of them do. If your child has a tough time with this, be there to encourage her and root her on. Don't grill her when she comes out of the audition room, asking what she could have done better. Just reassure her that as long as she gave it her all, that's all she can do. Help her put the audition behind her, and move on.

When your child doesn't get the job, tell her it's okay. Maybe they went with someone who was taller, shorter, fatter, thinner, more ethnic, less ethnic, etc. Let your child know that there could be a million reasons why the job went to someone else and that she shouldn't take it personally.

"If you're going to be supportive and make this move and make this sacrifice for your child, be supportive 100 percent of the time, especially before auditions," advises casting director Harriet Greenspan. "If your child doesn't think he did well, it's only one audition. They're children, they have their whole life ahead of them. Don't make them feel like this is it."

Agent Vivian Hollander offers her best advice for parents of younger actors. "My mantra is perspective," the talent rep reveals. "Perspective is the key to keeping success in check and not losing the child actor's identity. This is primarily the job of the parent. Protect your child from the negative influences."

"No matter how talented your child is, it's always going to be different," says Dianne Samonas, whose son Daniel plays recurring characters on *Entourage* and *Wizards of Waverly Place*. "Whatever you hear from other parents—take it with a grain of salt. Know it's not written in stone. If a lot of circumstances tend to fall into place, it means you're going in the right direction. If you keep hitting roadblocks and frustration, maybe it's not the right time. Listen to your instincts as a mother, and don't get caught up in the success stories of others. They're the exception, not the rule."

Roles of the Parent on Set

When your child does book the job, you will be with him on set as his de facto chaperone. This isn't your big opportunity to network—everyone there has a job to do. You do as well. You want to make sure your kid is always safe and accounted for while filming. Barring any unique production situations, your child should be within sight and earshot from you at all times.

Monitor your child's activity on set. Is he being asked to work overtime or more than the permitted number of hours for a child his age? Is he receiving meals and rest periods within the allotted times? Is he being taught in a designated classroom? Is the dressing room private and appropriate? Is he being asked to do anything you consider dangerous or inappropriate? If you have any concerns like the ones above, speak to the studio teacher, your handlers, or a union representative immediately.

I don't want to scare parents from enjoying the on-set experience, but you have to remember why you're there. Sure, you can be social and friendly, but don't approach the director while he's shooting to ask him what it was like working with the Olsen twins. Just as your child needs to maintain professionalism on set, so do you.

Being on set can become tedious after a while. It's not all the glitz and glamour you may imagine. Bring some books, or needlepoint, or Sudoku magazines to occupy your time. And if you've got younger child actors, make sure you have activities to occupy them, as well. When it's time for a meal, join the rest of the crew. If you get the munchies, head over to craft services. You don't need to hide in the trailer all day. My favorite on-set parents are the ones who are there to help their kids do a great job and are always friendly when approached.

"We might play games or talk or prepare for the next scene," says Mouser. "When they were younger, I kept things in my bag. We'd play tic-tac-toe, or I'd keep crayons and a sketch pad. Mary would go to town making pictures for the director and others on set. If I know they have a scene coming up, I get things ready so that when the kids finish with the teacher, they've got the material right there."

Tanya Harper tries to lay low when her son Shane is working on a project. "I usually read and take walks because I don't want to come off as 'one of those moms,'" says Harper. "We have a joke about it. Shane will say, 'Please don't be one of those moms'— the stage mom who doesn't ever go away and give room for the child to have his own space. It's a little bit scary. It doesn't look good for an actor. It could be a detriment to his career. So I literally go there with 'Don't be a stage mom' in my mind."

That said, Harper knows she has a right to be on set and an important role to fulfill while there. But she admits that sometimes the crew makes it seem like the parent has no business being on set. "They look at it as an inconvenience," says Harper. "By law, we're supposed to be there. There are sets where they don't want you there, so I try to stand as far back as possible, stay out of the way, and talk to the other moms and make friends."

"I don't know that everybody really understands the legality of it," Harper continues. "I've had sets where there literally wasn't a place for me to stand and one of the other moms pulled me in and said, 'You have a right to be here within view of your child.' But I always have apprehension when arriving on a new set. Are we going to be welcomed, or are we going to be looked at as a hassle?"

Moving On

As your child grows older, let her start to take a more proactive role in her business. I always like my clients to call me directly after an audition so I can hear their feedback firsthand. But as the kids grow up, I start talking to them more about their business as well, whereas before I'd reserve those conversations for the parents. Since you have your child's best interests at hand, encourage her to assume responsibility for her own career.

Believe it or not, handing over the reins of your child's career to her as she grows into a responsible adult isn't the hard part. It's suddenly finding yourself without a principal role in your child's professional life that can be difficult to swallow. After all, you've just devoted the better part of your life to nurturing that career—you've got a big gap to fill.

Just remember, even though your kids have grown up and don't need to rely on you as much for their business, you're still their parent. There will always be a special bond between parent and child, even if it's no longer on set. But sometimes parents have a difficult time moving on.

It's really no different than the empty-nest syndrome many parents experience when their kids head off to college. But because of all of that time you spent driving your child to and from auditions, and all of that time you spent with her on set while she was filming, the separation anxiety you experience could be more pronounced than you might expect.

This is why I always tell the parents of my kid actors, especially the ones who move to California to make this happen, you need to make a life for yourself out here, too. You've given up a lot, sacrificed your friends and the world you had built back home, to give your child an opportunity in this business. And ever since you moved to L.A., you've done nothing but support your child in this industry—both financially and emotionally.

When your child decides to flex his independence, and they all do, it's easy to see why it can be so hard letting go. But if you've got your own life, separate from your child and the business, it becomes much easier.

And be forewarned that your child could alert you at any time that he is done with this business. When kids get started at a particularly young age, they might just go with the flow. As they grow up, some discover that they don't want to be in this business, for whatever reason. Be okay with that.

"Parents need to let their kids know that it's about them," says Grant. "If at any point kids decide they don't want to do it anymore, make sure they know they have not failed. Better to find out now than later. Never be ashamed. Kids have it hard enough without that responsibility. We can always go back home. Help them understand that they don't have to stay in the business, because they don't."

I once had a client who worked all the time. But I could sense there were problems on the home front every time I spoke to his mom. They lived about an hour from L.A., and she'd complain that his dad didn't like them coming up to the city for auditions so often. It was creating genuine tension in their household.

My client, who was ten at the time, must have sensed this tension as well. He told his folks that he didn't want to be an actor anymore. I always thought that he did that to save his family and keep them together. And I told his mom that if he ever changed his mind, he'd always be welcomed back.

■ ■ ■

Being a parent to a showbiz kid really can be a full-time job. But remember, as in any field, when it's time to go home, leave the job at the office. Enjoy as much of a normal life as possible during your downtime.

"Don't get consumed by the biz," advises Samonas. "Don't sit by the phone waiting for calls. Keep busy with other interests in life: sports, friends, family . . . that's how you keep your sanity."

"Have a whole circle of friends outside the business," encourages agent Melissa Berger. "It's also important for kids to have someone to just play soccer with who isn't wondering what they've gone out on this week and then runs home to tell their mother what audition they should call their own agent about to get them in on."

Now that we're on our way, it's time to put it all together. The next chapter will discuss the difference between booking a job and building a career. We'll also explore how to find longevity in this business.

THE BIG PICTURE

This chapter shows you how to take everything we've discussed so far and put your game plan in motion. We'll explore how to manage your own career effectively and how to find longevity as an actor in this business. We'll consider when it's time to leave the youth market and start playing roles that are closer to your true age, and how to transition successfully from child star to adult actor.

The Luck Factor

If you've gotten this far, then you've certainly read a lot of information to help stack the odds in your favor. But there's another factor you need to consider: luck. Luck can play an integral part in one's success in this business.

I cannot predict what roles will be casting tomorrow. You might be the best actor in town, but if there isn't a role that is right for you, you're simply in the right place at the wrong time. How often have I heard feedback in which the casting director has told me that my client did an amazing job, but he's just not right for the part? Casting actors is not a science. In fact, it's completely subjective. You can give the performance of a lifetime on your next audition, but because you are a little too tall, or shorter than they envisioned, or remind the producer of his nephew Chad—but in a bad way—you just won't book the job.

You need to remain optimistic, however. Luck can also play greatly in your favor. You could actually wind up in the right place at the right time and book acting gigs on a regular basis. You could go in for a role that you're not even right for, but you might blow them away in the room, and the producers might change the role to fit you! A producer could think you stood out in your small role in his last film and you remind him of his nephew Chad—but in a good way—so he might decide to cast you in larger supporting roles in his next two projects.

So go on, roll the dice. Don't be afraid of what might not come. Instead, embrace this crazy business and make it work for you. And don't forget to have fun in the process, because if you're not enjoying it, why are you doing it?

"It's all about the stars aligning," says Abby Bluestone, head of the breakout division at Innovative Artists Agency. "You can be prepared, be the best one for the role, but they don't want you because you have brown hair or blue eyes."

"Right place, right time does play a part . . . but there is no substitution for consistency and preparedness," advises casting director Michelle Lewitt. "You improve your 'odds' of being successful if you are prepared for every opportunity that presents itself to you."

The Proactive Actor

If you work hard, give 100 percent, and do everything you can to make it, you will find some degree of success. That doesn't mean that you're going to be pulling down $20 million a movie. But success can be measured in many ways. Getting a callback equals success. Landing a role certainly means success. Seeing your face on the cover of a magazine might translate to success. Some successes come in even smaller packages: getting the perfect headshot, scoring an audition for your favorite show, and landing a meeting with a top talent representative are all positive steps in your career. Don't ignore all of the little successes along the way.

This business is constant. There's always something you can do to get better and move ahead. Whether it's perfecting your craft, networking with new contacts, or streamlining your business plan, being an actor is a lot more complex than simply walking the red carpet.

But you've got to be proactive about it. You can't just sit around and wait for auditions. Get yourself into a routine where you're actively doing something to move your career forward each day. At the end of each day, ask yourself,

"What did I do today to build my career?" If you can't answer that question every day, you're not being proactive enough.

"Continue to improve your craft and be prepared to hear constructive and not-so-constructive criticism," says Lewitt. "If you can take what people say and use it to improve, you will constantly be getting better and better. As fickle as this industry is, quality is quality no matter how you cut it. Become a quality actor who cares about your career and cares about being diligent in class and preparing for auditions. Work begets work."

Goals

Throughout your career, be sure to make a list of goals. These should include both short-term and long-term goals, and they should continually be updated. Short-term goals might include getting an agent, getting a callback, joining the union, or booking your first job. Long-term goals might include landing a lead in a blockbuster movie, getting a supporting role in a Sundance film, starting your own clothing line, or winning an Emmy.

Make your short-term goals attainable. Then carefully plan each step so you can achieve your objective. If getting an agent is your goal, your plan might be as follows:

1) Sign up for a showcase where you can perform for industry professionals seeking new talent.
2) Put together a list of potential agents.
3) Mail postcard-sized headshot invites to agents.
4) Follow up with agents who attend.

Long-term goals are usually achieved by completing a series of short-term goals. If your long-term goal is to land a role as a series regular on a pilot, your plan may be as follows:

1) Build an impressive resume with guest star credits on several TV shows.
2) Set general meetings with casting executives at the major networks.
3) Work with a coach before each pilot audition.

You can do everything right and still not achieve your goal. It happens. But you need to stay focused and remain positive. If at first you don't succeed, keep trying. Maybe there is a better plan than what you came up with originally. Periodically review your plans and your goals with your representation. Make sure that you're still on the same page. You can always ask them what else you could be doing to further your career.

Building a Career

It's one thing to book a job. It's another thing to build a successful career. So how do you turn a series of jobs into a career?

To build anything, you need to have a constant source of forward momentum. If you want to build a house, you lay a foundation, erect walls, and add a roof. Some parts of the process may take longer than others, but you never lose sight of your main objective, which is to build a home. You also don't go back to re-lay the foundation after the roof is on tight.

Actors want to work. And I want all of my clients to work. But I want them to make smart choices so that they can build a career and not just do a series of jobs. If you book several costar roles on major television shows, you're building a nice resume. But at some point, you will need to stop playing the costar parts and start booking the guest star roles. It's a hard transition to make. It could even mean saying no to costar work.

What actor in his right mind says no to work? An actor who is building a career, that's who. Big stars do it all the time. Sure, they have more leverage, but at that point in their careers, they try to make the right choices about the roles they play. Actors often turn down a large payday to work on a small independent film for little to no money. They do this because they feel these projects could stretch them artistically and really take their careers to new heights.

When I worked on the film *Mr. Wrong*, the lead male role was originally offered to Nicholas Cage. He turned it down, opting instead to take a role in a small independent film. That film was *Leaving Las Vegas*, and it won Cage his first Oscar.

When presented with an opportunity, a good question to ask yourself is, How will this role help my career? Not every job you take will advance your career. When you're just starting out, you will accept any job just to get yourself on the map. That's perfectly acceptable. But once you begin to make a name for yourself, the choices you make will affect your future to some extent. So make smart choices.

How to Manage Your Manager . . . As Well as the Rest of Your Team

At the start of this book, I wrote that you are the captain of the team. In essence, all of your handlers work for you. And while they are guiding and advising you, someone still needs to be team leader. That person is you.

As such, do you want to be the type of leader who sits around and gets told what to do or a leader who is an active part of the process of building your career? The latter consults with his team several times a week, keeps his agents in the loop by reporting back to them after his auditions, and communicates to his manager his honest concerns about forthcoming projects.

I'm not advocating telling your team how to do their job, especially since they've probably got a lot more experience in this business than you do when you're first starting out. But you need to feel comfortable and confident talking with them candidly about your career. And you should never feel like you're bothering them when you call, as long as you're calling about something of substance. But if you're calling several times a day with petty requests, this prevents them from allocating their time more beneficially toward advancing your career.

"Be in communication with your team and update us on everything from new classes, to haircuts, to every best friend that you have in high places," advises talent rep Bryan Leder. "Never be afraid to ask us questions. Remember that you are the ultimate decision maker, and we are always listening to you."

Growing Up and Out of the Youth Market

Let's face it: We all grow older and eventually look our age. For some, this happens quickly. Others are blessed with good genes and will continue to play young roles for years to come. (Thank you, Mom and Dad!) But at some point you'll need to transition out of playing kids and teens and into more mature parts.

Don't make this transition a hasty one. Once you start to age yourself on camera in terms of the roles you play, it's very difficult to go back to portraying the younger parts. For instance, if you're a twenty-eight-year-old woman who still looks like she's in high school, but you play a role in a new movie where you're the mother of nine-year-old twins, it's going to be awfully difficult to go back to playing an adolescent.

At the same time, if you want to move on from playing those high school roles, you absolutely should take on a more mature part. Playing the mother of nine-year-old twins would definitely help break you out of that mode. When we were casting *Frailty*, Bill Paxton had some reservations about taking on the role of Dad. He was concerned that playing the father of two young boys would age his image too much and limit his future acting possibilities. Obviously, he didn't need to be alarmed, as he continues to amaze us in a variety of fascinating roles on screen to this day. "It's the organic evolution," explains agent Abby Bluestone. "I've repped people for fifteen years. As they grow older, you just grow with them. There's no exact time to leave the youth market. All of a sudden, you're just older and moving on to more mature roles.

"At Innovative, we help them work on their careers, to cross into our [adult] talent department so they don't have to leave the agency," continues Bluestone. "They stay clients and stay with us. We just get other people involved organically and bring them onto the team."

The Long and Winding Road

There are no guarantees in Hollywood. It's not always easy to predict how long it will take until you book your first job . . . your next job . . . or if you'll be able to build enough momentum to truly launch into stardom.

This business can be funny at times. You may go an entire year without booking a single job. And then you may work steadily for two years in a row. You just cannot predict the unpredictable.

"My best advice to the young actor is to always enjoy the process and don't get caught up in the demands of parents or jealousies of others," suggests Vivian Hollander of Hollander Talent Group.

"Parents have to be really sure that this business is something the kids truly want to be part of," says Melissa Berger of CESD. "They have to want the process, and not because they want to see their face on the screen. You pay such a high price emotionally, mentally, financially, and time-wise, that it truly has to be your child's wish.

"And kids have to be aware of the sacrifice on the parents' part," Berger continues. "They give up a lot to take the child to classes, get the pictures, etc. It's a big commitment for the entire family. Everyone has to be onboard and really want to do it."

"Be honest with yourself. Why do you want to get into acting? Make yourself answer this question," says Lewitt. "Some of the wisest words ever spoken are from one of my favorite movies, *The Karate Kid*, where Mr. Miyagi says, 'Imagine you walking on road. You karate yes, safe. You karate no, safe. You karate guess so, squash just like grape.' Now insert the word acting for karate.

"If you get into this business, come into it 100 percent, or don't come in at all," Lewitt continues. "If you have any doubts or feelings of 'Eh, maybe,' you'll find yourself very unhappy on your journey. This business is for the strong-minded and talented. If your talents lie elsewhere, then go follow them. If acting is truly where your talents lie, then I hope to see you in my casting session very soon."

This may not be the easiest business in the world, but it can be very rewarding. The true reason to become an actor is because of your passion for the craft. As long as that passion remains strong, you can continue to act for as long as you breathe. And if this is your passion, don't ever let anyone tell you "No." Be persistent because if you can dream it, you can make it happen.

ACTORS WHO HAVE SUCCESSFULLY TRANSITIONED FROM CHILD STAR TO ADULT ACTOR

Sean Astin
Christian Bale
Drew Barrymore
Jason Bateman
Jennifer Connelly
Claire Danes
Matt Dillon
Kirsten Dunst
Jodie Foster
Judy Garland
Jackie Earle Haley
Helen Hunt
Scarlett Johansson
Roddy McDowell
Sarah Jessica Parker
Anna Paquin
Joaquin Phoenix
Natalie Portman
Christina Ricci
Mickey Rooney
Kurt Russell
Ricky Schroeder
Brooke Shields
Elizabeth Taylor
Elijah Wood
Natalie Wood

APPENDIX

NETWORKS

A&E
www.aetv.com

ABC
abc.go.com

ABC FAMILY
abcfamily.go.com

AMC
www.amctv.com

BET
www.bet.com

CARTOON NETWORK
www.cartoonnetwork.com

CBS
www.cbs.com

COMEDY CENTRAL
www.comedycentral.com

CW
www.cwtv.com

DISNEY CHANNEL
home.disney.go.com/tv

FOX
www.fox.com

FX
www.fxnetworks.com

HALLMARK
www.hallmarkchannel.com

HBO
www.hbo.com

LIFETIME
www.mylifetime.com

MTV
www.mtv.com

NBC
www.nbc.com

NICKELODEON
www.nick.com

SCI-FI
www.scifi.com

SHOWTIME
www.sho.com

SOAPNET
soapnet.go.com

STARZ
www.starz.com

THE N
www.the-n.com

TBS
www.tbs.com

TNT
www.tnt.tv

USA
www.usanetwork.com

STUDIOS

DISNEY
disney.go.com

DREAMWORKS
www.dreamworks.com

LIONS GATE
www.lionsgate.com

MGM
www.mgm.com

MIRAMAX
www.miramax.com

PARAMOUNT
www.paramount.com

SONY
www.sonypictures.com

TWENTIETH CENTURY FOX
www.foxmovies.com

UNIVERSAL
www.universalstudios.com

WARNER BROS.
www.warnerbros.com

THE WEINSTEIN COMPANY
www.weinsteinco.com

UNIONS

ACTORS' EQUITY ASSOCIATION (AEA)
www.actorsequity.org

ALLIANCE OF CANADIAN CINEMA, TELEVISION AND RADIO ARTISTS (ACTRA)
www.actra.ca

AMERICAN FEDERATION OF TELEVISION & RADIO ARTISTS (AFTRA)
www.aftra.org

SCREEN ACTORS GUILD (SAG)
www.sag.org

READING LIST

Belli, Mary Lou, and Dinah Lenney. 2006. *Acting for Young Actors*. New York: Back Stage Books.

LeMack, Brad. 2002. *The Business of Acting*. Los Angeles: Ingenuity Press.

Levy, Frederick. 2000. *Hollywood 101: The Film Industry*. New York: St. Martin's.

Levy, Frederick. 2008. *15 Minutes of Fame: Becoming a Star in the YouTube Revolution*. New York: Alpha/Penguin.

Lewis, M. K., and Rosemary Lewis. 1997. *Your Film Acting Career*. Santa Monica, CA: Gorham House.

Lukeman, Noah. 2002. *The Plot Thickens*. New York: St. Martin's.

Sedita, Scott. 2006. *The Eight Characters of Comedy*. Los Angeles: Atides.

Sedita, Scott. 2008. *Scott Sedita's Guide to Making It in Hollywood: 3 Steps to Success, 3 Steps to Failure*. Los Angeles: Atides.

ADDITIONAL WEBSITES

The Futon Critic: www.thefutoncritic.com
Internet Broadway Database: www.ibdb.com
Internet Movie Database: www.imdb.com, www.imdbpro.com
Professional Actors Resource Forum:
   forums.delphiforums.com/proactors

AGENCIES

The following list contains all types of agencies. Some represent children exclusively, others represent only adults, and still others represent kids and adults. I've included them all because adults who play young might find representation with both an adult agency and a youth agency. It's always a good idea to Google the name of the agency you're interested in to find information about them online.

ABOUT ARTISTS AGENCY
1650 Broadway
Suite 1406
New York, NY 10017
Phone: (212) 581-1857
www.aboutartistsagency.com

ABRAMS ARTISTS AGENCY
9200 Sunset Blvd., #1130
Los Angeles, CA 90069
Phone: (310) 859-0625
www.abramsartists.com

ABRAMS ARTISTS AGENCY (NY)
275 Seventh Ave.
26th Floor
New York, NY 10001
Phone: (646) 486-4600
www.abramsartists.com

ACCESS TALENT
171 Madison Ave.
Suite 910
New York, NY 10016
Phone: (212) 684-7795
www.accesstalent.com

AGENCY FOR THE PERFORMING ARTS (APA)
405 S. Beverly Dr.
Beverly Hills, CA 90212
Phone: (310) 888-4200
www.apa-agency.com

AGENCY FOR THE PERFORMING ARTS (NASHVILLE)
3017 Poston Ave.
Nashville, TN 37203
Phone: (615) 297-0100
www.apanashville.com

AGENCY FOR THE PERFORMING ARTS (NY)
250 W. 57th St. #1701
New York, NY 10107
Phone: (212) 687-0092
www.apanewyork.com

AKA TALENT AGENCY
6310 San Vicente Blvd., #200
Los Angeles, CA 90048
Phone: (323) 965-5600
www.akatalent.com

ALVARADO REY AGENCY

7906 Santa Monica Blvd.
Suite 205
West Hollywood, CA 90046
Phone: (323) 656-2277
www.alvaradorey.com

AMSEL-EISENSTADT & FRAZIER

5055 Wilshire Blvd., #865
Los Angeles, CA 90036
Phone: (323) 939-1188

ANDREADIS TALENT

119 W. 57th St.
Suite 711
New York, NY 10019
Phone: (212) 315-0303

ANGEL CITY TALENT

4741 Laurel Canyon Blvd., #101
Valley Village, CA 91607
Phone: (818) 760-9980
www.angelcitytalent.biz

ANN STEELE AGENCY

330 W. 42nd St.
18th Floor
New York, NY 10036
Phone: (212) 629-9112

ARCIERI & ASSOCIATES

305 Madison Ave., #2315
New York, NY 10165
Phone: (212) 286-1700
www.arcieritalent.com

**ARTISTS ENTERTAINMENT
AGENCY, LLC**

165 W. 46th St., #1114
New York, NY 10036
Phone: (212) 869-7093
www.artistsentertainment
agency.com

ATLAS TALENT AGENCY

15 E. 32nd St.
6th Floor
New York, NY 10016
Phone: (212) 730-4500

AVALON ARTISTS GROUP

5455 Wilshire Blvd., #1111
Los Angeles, CA 90036
Phone: (323) 692-1700
www.avalonartists.com

BARBAZON AGENCY

7535 East Hampden Ave. #108
Denver, CO 80231
Phone: (303) 337-7954

BAUMAN-REDANTY & SHAUL

5757 Wilshire Blvd., #473
Los Angeles, CA 90036
Phone: (323) 857-6666

BAUMAN-REDANTY & SHAUL (NY)

1650 Broadway, #1410
New York, NY 10019
Phone: (212) 757-0098

BEACON TALENT AGENCY, INC.

9255 Sunset Blvd.
Suite 727
Los Angeles, CA 90069
Phone: (310) 278-1900

BEVERLY AGENCY, THE

20501 Ventura Blvd.
Suite 210
Woodland Hills, CA 91364
Phone: (818) 660-2122
www.thebeverlyagencyinc.com

BEVERLY HECHT AGENCY

3500 W. Olive Ave., #1180
Burbank, CA 91505
Phone: (818) 505-1192
www.beverlyhecht.com

BOBBY BALL AGENCY

4605 Lankershim Blvd., #721
Universal City, CA 91602
Phone: (818) 506-8188
www.bobbyballagency.com

BRADY, BRANNON, RICH

5670 Wilshire Blvd., #820
Los Angeles, CA 90036
Phone: (323) 852-9559

BRESLER-KELLY & ASSOCIATES

11500 W. Olympic Blvd., #352
Los Angeles, CA 90064
Phone: (310) 479-5611

BRET ADAMS LTD.

448 W. 44th St.
New York, NY 10036
Phone: (212) 765-5630
www.bretadamsltd.net

BROGAN AGENCY, THE

1517 Park Row
Venice, CA 90291
Phone: (310) 450-9700
www.thebroganagency.com

DON BUCHWALD & ASSOCIATES

6500 Wilshire Blvd., #2200
Los Angeles, CA 90048
Phone: (323) 655-7400
www.buchwald.com

DON BUCHWALD & ASSOCIATES (NY)

10 E. 44th St.
New York, NY 10017
Phone: (212) 867-1200
www.buchwald.com

CARSON ORGANIZATION

419 Park Ave. South, #606
New York, NY 10016
Phone: (212) 221-1517

CARSON-ADLER AGENCY

250 W. 57th St.
Suite 808
New York, NY 10107
Phone: (212) 307-1882
www.carsonadler.com

CIRCLE TALENT ASSOC.

433 N. Camden Dr., #400
Beverly Hills, CA 90210
Phone: (310) 279-5155

CLEAR TALENT GROUP

10950 Ventura Blvd.
Studio City, CA 91604
Phone: (818) 509-0121
www.cleartalentgroup.com

CLEAR TALENT GROUP (NY)

325 West 38th St.
Suite 1203
New York, NY 10018
Phone: (212) 840-4100
www.cleartalentgroup.com

CLI

843 North Sycamore Ave.
Los Angeles, CA 90038
Phone: (323) 461-3971

COAST TO COAST TALENT GROUP

3350 Barham Blvd.
Los Angeles, CA 90068
Phone: (323) 845-9200
www.ctctalent.com

COMMERCIAL TALENT INC.

9255 Sunset Blvd., #505
Los Angeles, CA 90069
Phone: (310) 247-1431

COMMERCIALS UNLIMITED INC.

190 N. Canon Dr., #302
Beverly Hills, CA 90210
Phone: (310) 278-5123

CORNERSTONE TALENT AGENCY

37 W. 20th St., #1108
New York, NY 10011
Phone: (212) 807-8344

CORSA AGENCY, THE

11704 Wilshire Blvd.
Suite 204
Los Angeles, CA 90025
Phone: (310) 231-7010

CRAIG WYCKOFF & ASSOCIATES

11350 Ventura Blvd., #100
Studio City, CA 91604
Phone: (818) 752-2300

CREATIVE ARTISTS AGENCY (CAA)

2000 Avenue of the Stars
Los Angeles, CA 90067
Phone: (424) 288-2000
www.caa.com

CREATIVE ARTISTS AGENCY (CAA) (NY)

162 Fifth Ave.
6th Floor
New York, NY 10010
Phone: (212) 833-3600
www.caa.com

CREATIVE ARTISTS AGENCY (CAA) (NASHVILLE)

3310 West End Ave.
3rd Floor
Nashville, TN 37203
Phone: (615) 383-8787

THE CULBERTSON GROUP

8430 Santa Monica Blvd., #210
West Hollywood, CA 90069
Phone: (323) 650-9454

CUNNINGHAM-ESCOTT-SLEVIN-DOHERTY

10635 Santa Monica Blvd.
Los Angeles, CA 90025
Phone: (310) 475-2111
www.cesdtheatrical.com
www.cesdvoices.com
www.cesdanimation.com

CUNNINGHAM-ESCOTT-SLEVIN-DOHERTY (NY)

257 Park Avenue South, #900
New York, NY 10010
Phone: (212) 477-1666
www.cesdtheatrical.com
www.cesdvoices.com
www.cesdanimation.com

DPN TALENT AGENCY

9201 W. Olympic Blvd.
Beverly Hills, CA 90212
Phone: (310) 432-7800
www.dpntalent.com

DANIEL HOFF TALENT AGENCY

5455 Wilshire Blvd., #1100
Los Angeles, CA 90036
Phone: (323) 932-2500
www.danielhoffagency.com

DEFINING ARTISTS

10 Universal City Plaza, #2000
Universal City, CA 91608
Phone: (818) 753-2405
www.definingartists.com

DIVERSE TALENT GROUP

1875 Century Park East, #2250
Los Angeles, CA 90067
Phone: (310) 201-6565
www.diversetalentgroup.com

DOMAIN

9229 Sunset Blvd., #415
West Hollywood, CA 90069
Phone: (310) 888-8500

DOUGLAS-GORMAN-ROTHACKER & WILHELM (DGRW)

1501 Broadway
Suite 703
New York, NY 10036
Phone: (212) 382-2000
www.dgrwinc.com

ENDEAVOR AGENCY

9601 Wilshire Blvd.
3rd Floor
Beverly Hills, CA 90212
Phone: (310) 248-2000

ENDEAVOR AGENCY (NY)

23 Watts
6th Floor
New York, NY 10013
Phone: (212) 625-2500

FIFI OSCARD AGENCY

110 W. 40th St.
Suite 2100
New York, NY 10018
Phone: (212) 764-1100
www.fifioscard.com

FORTITUDE TALENT AGENCY

8619 Washington Blvd.
Culver City, CA 90232
Phone: (310) 300-4073

**FRONTIER BOOKING
INTERNATIONAL**

1560 Broadway
Suite 1110
New York, NY 10036
Phone: (212) 221-0220
www.frontierbooking.com

GAGE GROUP, THE

14724 Ventura Blvd., #505
Sherman Oaks, CA 91403
Phone: (818) 905-3800

GAGE GROUP, THE (NY)

450 Seventh Ave., #1809
New York, NY 10123
Phone: (212) 541-5250

GERSH AGENCY, THE

232 North Canon Dr.
Beverly Hills, CA 90210
Phone: (310) 274-6611
www.gershagency.com

**GERSH AGENCY,
THE (NY)**

41 Madison Ave.
33rd Floor
New York, NY 10010
Phone: (212) 997-1818
www.gershagency.com

GLICK AGENCY, THE

1250 6th St., #100
Santa Monica, CA 90401
Phone: (310) 593-6500

GLOBAL ARTISTS AGENCY

6253 Hollywood Blvd., #508
Hollywood, CA 90028
Phone: (323) 836-0320
www.globalartistsagency.net

GVA TALENT AGENCY

9229 Sunset Blvd., #320
Los Angeles, CA 90069
Phone: (310) 278-1310

GWYN FOXX TALENT AGENCY

3500 W. Olive Ave., Suite 300
Burbank, CA 91505
Phone: (818) 973-2732

HARDEN-CURTIS

850 Seventh Ave.
Suite 903
New York, NY 10019
Phone: (212) 977-8502
www.hardencurtis.com

HARTIG-HILEPO AGENCY

54 W. 21st St.
Suite 610
New York, NY 10010
Phone: (212) 929-1772

HENDERSON/HOGAN AGENCY

850 Seventh Ave.
Suite 1003
New York, NY 10019
Phone: (212) 765-5190

HERB TANNEN & ASSOC.

20520 Pinnacle Way
Malibu, CA 90265
Phone: (310) 446-5802

HOUSE OF REPRESENTATIVES, THE

1434 6th St., #3
Santa Monica, CA 90401
Phone: (310) 451-2345

HOWARD TALENT WEST

10657 Riverside Dr.
Toluca Lake, CA 91602
Phone: (818) 766-5300

IMPERIUM 7

9911 W. Pico Blvd., #1290
Los Angeles, CA 90035
Phone: (310) 203-9009

INDEPENDENT ARTISTS AGENCY, INC.

9601 Wilshire Blvd.
Suite 750
Beverly Hills, CA 90210
Phone: (310) 550-5000

INNOVATIVE ARTISTS

1505 10th St.
Santa Monica, CA 90401
Phone: (310) 656-0400
www.innovativeartists.com

INNOVATIVE ARTISTS (NY)

235 Park Avenue South
10th Floor
New York, NY 10003
Phone: (212) 253-6900
www.innovativeartists.com

INTERNATIONAL CREATIVE MANAGEMENT (ICM)

10250 Constellation Blvd.
Los Angeles, CA 90067
Phone: (310) 550-4000
www.icmtalent.com

INTERNATIONAL CREATIVE MANAGEMENT (NY)

825 Eighth Ave.
26th Floor
New York, NY 10019
Phone: (212) 556-5600
www.icmtalent.com

JKA TALENT & LITERARY

12725 Ventura Blvd., #H
Studio City, CA 91604
Phone: (818) 980-2093

JORDAN-GILL & DORNBAUM

1133 Broadway
Suite 623
New York, NY 10010
Phone: (212) 463-8455

JUDY BOALS INC.—A TALENT AND LITERARY AGENCY

307 W. 38th St., #812
New York, NY 10018
Phone: (212) 500-1424
www.judyboals.com

JUDY SCHOEN & ASSOC.

606 N. Larchmont Blvd. #309
Los Angeles, CA 90004
Phone: (323) 962-1950

KAZARIAN/SPENCER/RUSKIN & ASSOC.

11969 Ventura Blvd.
3rd Floor, Box 7409
Studio City, CA 91604
Phone: (818) 769-9111
www.ksawest.com

KAZARIAN/SPENCER/ RUSKIN (NY)

Media Arts Building
11 W. 43rd St., #1107
New York, NY 10036
Phone: (212) 582-7572
www.ksawest.com

KERIN-GOLDBERG ASSOCIATES

155 E. 55th St.
Suite 5D
New York, NY 10022
Phone: (212) 838-7373

KOHNER AGENCY, THE

9300 Wilshire Blvd. #555
Beverly Hills, CA 90212
Phone: (310) 550-1060

KOLSTEIN TALENT AGENCY

247 W. 38th St., #1001
New York, NY 10018
Phone: (212) 937-8967
www.kolsteintalent.com

KRASNY OFFICE, THE

1501 Broadway #1303
New York, NY 10036
Phone: (212) 730-8160

L.A. TALENT, INC.

7700 Sunset Blvd.
Los Angeles, CA 90046
Phone: (323) 436-7777
www.latalent.com

LALLY TALENT AGENCY

630 Ninth Ave.
Suite 800
New York, NY 10036
Phone: (212) 974-8718

LEADING ARTISTS, INC.

145 W. 45th St.
Suite 1000
New York, NY 10036
Phone: (212) 391-4545

MAVRICK ARTISTS AGENCY

1680 North Vine St., #802
Hollywood, CA 90028
Phone: (323) 382-0620
www.mavrickartists.com

MCCABE GROUP

8285 Sunset Blvd., #1
Los Angeles, CA 90046
Phone: (323) 650-3738
www.atalentagency.com

MCDONALD SELZNICK

1611 A N. El Centro Ave.
Los Angeles, CA 90028
Phone: (323) 957-6680
www.mcdonaldselznick.com

METROPOLITAN TALENT AGENCY

4500 Wilshire Blvd.
2nd Floor
Los Angeles, CA 90010
Phone: (323) 857-4500
www.mta.com

THE MINE

135 W. 27th St.
9th Floor
New York, NY 10001
Phone: (212) 612-3200

MITCHELL K. STUBBS & ASSOC.

8675 W. Washington Blvd., #203
Culver City, CA 90232
Phone: (310) 838-1200
www.mksagency.com

MOMENTUM TALENT AGENCY

6399 Wilshire Blvd.
Suite 1010
Los Angeles, CA 90048
Phone: (323) 951-1151
www.momentumtal.com

MORGAN AGENCY, THE

1200 N. Doheny Dr.
Los Angeles, CA 90069
Phone: (310) 860-0530
www.themorganagency.com

NATHE & ASSOCIATES

8281 Melrose Ave., #200
Los Angeles, CA 90046
Phone: (323) 653-7573

NICOLOSI & COMPANY

150 W. 25th St., #1200
New York, NY 10001
Phone: (212) 633-1010

OSBRINK TALENT AGENCY

4343 Lankershim Blvd., #100
Universal City, CA 91602
Phone: (818) 760-2488
www.osbrinkagency.com

PAKULA/KING & ASSOCIATES

9229 Sunset Blvd., #315
Los Angeles, CA 90069
Phone: (310) 281-4868

PANTHEON

1900 Avenue of the Stars, #2840
Los Angeles, CA 90067
Phone: (310) 201-0120

PARADIGM

360 N. Crescent Dr.
N. Building
Beverly Hills, CA 90210
Phone: (310) 288-8000
www.paradigmagency.com

PARADIGM (NY)

360 Park Avenue South
16th Floor
New York, NY 10010
Phone: (212) 703-7540
www.paradigmagency.com

**PEOPLE STORE &
HOT SHOT KIDS**

645 Lambert Dr.
Atlanta, GA 30324
Phone: (404) 874-6448
www.peoplestore.net

PETER STRAIN & ASSOC.

5455 Wilshire Blvd., #1812
Los Angeles, CA 90036
Phone: (323) 525-3391

PETER STRAIN & ASSOC. (NY)

321 W. 44th St., #805
New York, NY 10036
Phone: (212) 391-0380

PHOENIX ARTISTS AGENCY

321 W. 44th St.
Suite 401
New York, NY 10036
Phone: (212) 586-9110

PINNACLE COMMERCIAL TALENT

5757 Wilshire Blvd., #510
Los Angeles, CA 90036
Phone: (323) 939-5440

PROGRESSIVE ARTISTS AGENCY

1041 North Formosa Ave.
Formosa Bldg, #194
Los Angeles, CA 90046
Phone: (323) 850-2992

RAGE MODELS & TALENT

23679 Calabasas Rd.
Suite 501
Calabasas, CA 91302
Phone: (818) 225-0526
www.ragemodels.com

**REBEL ENTERTAINMENT
PARTNERS INC.**

5700 Wilshire Blvd.
Suite 456
Los Angeles, CA 90036
Phone: (323) 935-1700
www.reptalent.com

SAVAGE AGENCY

6212 Banner Ave.
Hollywood, CA 90038
Phone: (323) 461-8316

SBV TALENT

145 South Fairfax Ave., #310
Los Angeles, CA 90036
Phone: (323) 938-6000
www.sbvtalentagency.com

**SCHIOWITZ CONNOR
ANKRUM WOLF**

165 W. 46th St.
Suite 1210
New York, NY 10036
Phone: (212) 840-6787

SMS TALENT INC.

8730 Sunset Blvd., #440
Los Angeles, CA 90069
Phone: (310) 289-0909

**SPECIAL ARTISTS
AGENCY**

9465 Wilshire Blvd., #890
Beverly Hills, CA 90212
Phone: (310) 859-9688

STARS: THE AGENCY

23 Grant Ave.
4th Floor
San Francisco, CA 94108
Phone: (415) 421-6272
www.starsagency.com

STEWART TALENT AGENCY

1560 Broadway
10th Floor
New York, NY 10036
Phone: (212) 201-3590
www.stewarttalent.com

STONE MANNERS A TALENT & LITERARY AGENCY

9911 West Pico Blvd.
Suite 1400
Los Angeles, CA 90035
Phone: (323) 655-1313

STONE MANNERS A TALENT & LITERARY AGENCY (NY)

900 Broadway, #803
New York, NY 10003
Phone: (212) 505-1400

SYNERGY TALENT AGENCY

13251 Ventura Blvd., #2
Studio City, CA 91604
Phone: (818) 995-6500

TALENT HOUSE, THE

325 W. 38th St., #605
New York, NY 10018
Phone: (212) 957-5220

TALENT NETWORK GROUP

381 Park Ave. South
15th Floor
New York, NY 10016
Phone: (212) 889-1613

TALENT REPRESENTATIVES

307 E. 44th St., #1F
New York, NY 10017
Phone: (212) 752-1835

TALENTWORKS

3500 West Olive Ave., #1400
Burbank, CA 91505
Phone: (818) 972-4300
www.talentworks.us

TALENTWORKS (NY)

220 E. 23rd St., #400
New York, NY 10010
Phone: (212) 889-0800
www.talentworks.us

UGLY TALENT AGENCY

37 W. 26th St.
Suite 1208
New York, NY 10010
Phone: (212) 211-9237
www.uglyny.com

UNITED TALENT AGENCY (UTA)

9560 Wilshire Blvd.
5th Floor
Beverly Hills, CA 90212
Phone: (310) 273-6700
www.unitedtalent.com

VENTURE I.A.B., INC.

2509 Wilshire Blvd.
Los Angeles, CA 90057
Phone: (213) 381-1900
www.ventureinfonetwork.com

VISION TALENT

8500 Steller Dr., #8
Culver City, CA 90232
Phone: (310) 733-4420

VOX, INC.

5670 Wilshire Blvd., #820
Los Angeles, CA 90036
Phone: (323) 655-8699

WILLIAM MORRIS AGENCY, LLC

One William Morris Place
Beverly Hills, CA 90212
Phone: (310) 859-4000
www.wma.com

WILLIAM MORRIS AGENCY, LLC (MIAMI)

119 Washington Ave., #400
Miami Beach, FL 33139
Phone: (305) 938-2000
www.wma.com

WILLIAM MORRIS AGENCY, LLC (NASHVILLE)

2100 West End Ave., #1000
Nashville, TN 37203
Phone: (615) 385-0310
www.wma.com

WILLIAM MORRIS AGENCY, LLC (NY)

1325 Avenue of the Americas
New York, NY 10019
Phone: (212) 586-5100
www.wma.com

MANAGEMENT FIRMS

This is a list of management companies. Some exclusively represent young talent, others only manage adult actors, and there are also those that represent talent of all ages. As with agencies, it's always best to do your homework and find out as much as you can about each management firm before pursuing them for representation.

3 ARTS ENTERTAINMENT
9450 Wilshire Blvd.
7th Floor
Beverly Hills, CA 90212
(310) 888-3200

A WINK AND A NOD PRODUCTIONS
843 Twelfth St. #4
Santa Monica, CA 90403
(310) 394-5752
www.awinkandanod.com

ABSOLUTE TALENT
9713 Santa Monica Blvd., #219
Beverly Hills, CA 90210
(310) 273-1373
www.absolutetalent.net

ALLMAN-REA MANAGEMENT
9255 Sunset Blvd.
Suite #600
Los Angeles, CA 90069
(310) 440-5780
www.allmanrea.com

AMERICAN ARTISTS
13321 Ventura Blvd.
Suite C
Sherman Oaks, CA 91423
(818) 501-8917
americanartists@earthlink.net

ANDREA SIMON ENTERTAINMENT
4230 Woodman Ave.
Sherman Oaks, CA 91423
(818) 380-1901
www.andreasimonent.com

ANONYMOUS CONTENT
3532 Hayden Ave.
Culver City, CA 90232
(310) 558-6000
www.anonymouscontent.com

APRIL MILLS ENTERTAINMENT
PO Box 1983
Burbank, CA 91507
(818) 667-9529
aprilmillsentertainment.com

ARTISTRY ENTERTAINMENT

340 N. Camden Dr.
Suite 203
Beverly Hills, CA 90210
(310) 659-4044

**ARTS AND LETTERS
ENTERTAINMENT**

7715 Sunset Blvd.
Suite 100
Los Angeles, CA 90046
(323) 883-1070
www.artsandlets.com

AUDREY CAAN MANAGEMENT

8665 Burton Way
Suite 520
Los Angeles, CA 90048
(310) 273-7044

BAMBOO MANAGEMENT

17 Buccaneer St.
Marina Del Rey, CA 90292
(310) 827-0930
bamboo@ca.rr.com

BARRY KROST MANAGEMENT

9229 Sunset Blvd.
Suite 215
Los Angeles, CA 90069
(310) 278-8161

BEDDINGFIELD COMPANY, THE

13600 Ventura Blvd.
Suite B
Sherman Oaks, CA 91423
(818) 285-7411
rbedd@aol.com

BENSKY ENTERTAINMENT

15030 Ventura Blvd.
Suite 303
Sherman Oaks, CA 91403
(818) 830-3912
lynbensky@aol.com

**BETH COLT (GATEWAY
MANAGEMENT PARTNERS)**

5225 Wilshire Blvd.
Suite 702
Los Angeles, CA 90036
(323) 935-4141

BILL SILVA MANAGEMENT

8225 Santa Monica Blvd.
West Hollywood, CA 90046
(310) 651-3310
www.billsilvaentertainment.com

BILLY MILLER MANAGEMENT

8322 Ridpath Dr.
Los Angeles, CA 90046
(323) 822-0522
billymillermgmt@aol.com

BLACK ORCHID ENTERTAINMENT

7095 Hollywood Blvd.
Hollywood, CA 90028
(323) 962-9501
www.blackorchident.com

BRAVERMAN/BLOOM

14320 Ventura Blvd.
Suite 632
Sherman Oaks, CA 91423
(818) 459-3900

BRILLSTEIN GRAY

9150 Wilshire Blvd.
Suite 350
Beverly Hills, CA 90212
(310) 275-6135

BROWN LEADER MANAGEMENT GROUP

3000 Olympic Blvd.
Suite 1302
Santa Monica, CA 90404
(310) 315-4804
philip@brownleadergroup.com

BRYAN LEDER TALENT

227 Riverside Dr.
Suite 6E
New York, NY 10025
(917) 912-7564
bryan@bltmanagement.com

BURT SHAPIRO

2147 N. Beachwood Dr.
Los Angeles, CA 90058
(323) 469-9452
www.burtshapiro.com
burtjay@mail.com

C. SCHORR MANAGEMENT

4378 Sepulveda Blvd.
Suite 405
Sherman Oaks, CA 91403
(818) 788-1312

CALLIOPE TALENT MANAGEMENT

101 N. Victory Blvd.
Suite L267
Burbank, CA 91502
(323) 343-9823
www.calliopetalent.com

CAZZ MANAGEMENT

62 Haynes Ave.
West Islip, NY 11795
(631) 889-2423
www.cazzmanagement.com

CONTEMPORARY TALENT PARTNERS

1800 Century Park East
Suite 600
Los Angeles, CA 90067
(310) 365-5485
dondi_1@yahoo.com

COPPAGE COMPANY, THE

11902 Ventura Blvd.
Suite 147
Studio City, CA 91604
(818) 980-8806
coppage@aol.com

CORNER OF THE SKY ENTERTAINMENT

1635 N. Cahuenga Blvd.
Los Angeles, CA 90028
(323) 860-1572
www.cornerofthesky.com

DANIEL ROJO ENTERTAINMENT

269 S. Beverly Dr., #486
Beverly Hills, CA 90212
(323) 852-0082
rojomgmt@aol.com

DAVID MARTIN MANAGEMENT

13849 Riverside Dr.
Sherman Oaks, CA 91423
(818) 981-8686
davidmartinmgmnt@aol.com

DCA PRODUCTIONS

(800) 659-2063
www.dcaproductions.com

**DOLORES ROBINSON
ENTERTAINMENT**

3815 Hughes Ave.
3rd Floor
Culver City, CA 90232
(310) 777-8777
dolores@drobinsonent.com

DREAMSCOPE ENTERTAINMENT

211 North Valley St.
Burbank, CA 91505
(818) 558-1200

ELEMENTS ENTERTAINMENT

1635 N. Cahuenga Blvd.
5th Floor
Los Angeles, CA 90028
(323) 860-1565

ENTERTAINMENT GROUP, THE

292 Fifth Ave.
4th Floor
New York, NY 10001
(646) 485-7684
merrittb@optonline.net

**ESTELLE HERTZBERG
MANAGEMENT**

6242 Tunney Ave.
Tarzana, CA 91335
(818) 521-1660

FLASHPOINT ENTERTAINMENT

9150 Wilshire Blvd.
Suite 247
Beverly Hills, CA 90212
(310) 205-6300

FLUTIE ENTERTAINMENT

9595 Wilshire Blvd.
Suite 900
Beverly Hills, CA 90272
(310) 247-1100
pbrown@llutieent.com

FORSTER ENTERTAINMENT

12533 Woodgreen St.
Bldg. B
Los Angeles, CA 90066
(310) 636-4477
afoent@aol.com

FRANCHOT MANAGEMENT

PO Box 48890A
Los Angeles, CA 90048
(323) 954-9024
franman84@sbcglobal.net

FULL CIRCLE MANAGEMENT

(818) 769-2200

GAIL ABBOTT MANAGEMENT

3019 Hollycrest Dr.
Los Angeles, CA 90068
(323) 876-6868
gamngmnt@aol.com

GENDECE ENTERTAINMENT GROUP

238 14th St.
Seal Beach, CA 90740
(818) 623-9242
www.gendece.com

GRADE A ENTERTAINMENT

149 S. Barrington Ave.
Suite 719
Los Angeles, CA 90049
(310) 358-8600
development@gradeaent.com

GREEN KEY MANAGEMENT

251 West 89th St.
Suite 4-A
New York, NY 10024
(212) 874-7373
www.greenkeymanagement.com

HASSMAN ENTERTAINMENT

11601 Dunstan Way
Suite 206
Brentwood, CA 90049
(310) 471-4546
www.hassman.com

HEIDI ROTBART MANAGEMENT

1810 Malcolm Ave.
Suite 207
Los Angeles, CA 90025
(310) 470-8339
rotbartmgt@aol.com

HINES & HUNT

1213 W. Magnolia Blvd.
Burbank, CA 91506
(818) 557-7516

HOLLY LEBED PERSONAL MANAGEMENT

The Wilshire Marquis
10535 Wilshire Blvd.
Suite 808
Los Angeles, CA 90024
(310) 701-4712
kcadi@aol.com

INCOGNITO ENTERTAINMENT

8265 West Sunset Blvd.
Suite 100
West Hollywood, CA 90046
(323) 993-7370
entertainmentincognito@
yahoo.com

INDUSTRY ENTERTAINMENT

955 Carrillo Dr.
Suite 300
Los Angeles, CA 90048
(323) 954-9000

JAMES/LEVY MANAGEMENT

3500 West Olive Ave.
Suite 1470
Burbank, CA 91505
(818) 955-7070

JAN MAXWELL SMITH

(818) 528-7735

JEFF MORRONE TALENT MANAGEMENT

9350 Wilshire Blvd.
Suite 224
Beverly Hills, CA 90212
(310) 271-0019

JEFF ROSS ENTERTAINMENT
14560 Benefit St.
Suite 206
Sherman Oaks, CA 91403
(818) 788-6847

JEFF WALD ENTERTAINMENT
176 Acari Dr.
Los Angeles, CA 90049
(310) 472-9797

JOAN GREEN MANAGEMENT
1836 Courtney Terrace
Los Angeles, CA 90046
(323) 878-0484

JOANNE HOROWITZ MANAGEMENT
9350 Wilshire Blvd.
Suite 224
Beverly Hills, CA 90212
(310) 271-0719

KANNER ENTERTAINMENT
30 W. 74th Street, PH 1
New York, NY 10023
(212) 496-8175
kannerent@gmail.com

KASS & STOKES MANAGEMENT
9229 Sunset Blvd.
Suite 504
Los Angeles, CA 90069
(310) 385-8500

KERNER MANAGEMENT ASSOCIATES
311 N. Robertson Blvd.
Suite 288
Beverly Hills, CA 90211
(323) 658-9180

KINGS HIGHWAY ENTERTAINMENT
14538 Benefit St.
Suite 103
Sherman Oaks, CA 91423
(818) 981-2611

L. RICHARDSON ENTERTAINMENT
4570 Van Nuys Blvd.
Suite 432
Sherman Oaks, CA 91403
(818) 990-4706

LANE MANAGEMENT GROUP
13017 Woodbridge St.
Studio City, CA 91604
(818) 990-6366
www.lanemanagement.com

LAUGH FACTORY INC.
8001 Sunset Blvd.
West Hollywood, CA 90046
(323) 848-2800
www.laughfactory.com

LEFT COAST MUSIC GROUP
(818) 435-2203
www.leftcoastmusicgroup.com

LEMACK & COMPANY

2275 Huntington Dr.
Suite 552
San Marino, CA 91108
(626) 285-4040
www.lemackco.com

LESHER ENTERTAINMENT

(323) 932-9898

**LIBERMAN-ZERMAN
MANAGEMENT**

252 N. Larchmont Blvd.
Suite 200
Los Angeles, CA 90004
(323) 464-0870

LIGHTHOUSE ENTERTAINMENT

409 North Camden Dr.
Suite 202
Beverly Hills, CA 90210
(310) 246-0499
asst@lighthousela.com

LINDA REITMAN MANAGEMENT

820 North San Vicente Blvd.
Box 691736
Los Angeles, CA 90069
(323) 852-9091

**LUBER ROCKLAND
ENTERTAINMENT**

8530 Wilshire Blvd.
Suite 550
Beverly Hills, CA 90211
(310) 289-1088

**MAGENTA CREATIVE
MANAGEMENT**

9 North Moore St.
New York, NY 10013
(212) 226-7677
magentamgt@gmail.com

MAGGIE SMITH MANAGEMENT

3365 Paseo Del Sol
Calabasas, CA 91302
(818) 591-7665
maggiesmithmgmt@
adelphia.net

MAIN TITLE ENTERTAINMENT

5225 Wilshire Blvd.
Suite 500
Los Angeles, CA 90036
(323) 964-9900

MANAGEMENT 101

5527 1/2 Cahuenga Blvd.
North Hollywood, CA 91601
(818) 753-5200

MANAGEMENT 360

9111 Wilshire Blvd.
Beverly Hills,
CA 90210
(310) 272-7000

MAPLE JAM MUSIC GROUP

www.maplejammusic.com

MARATHON ENTERTAINMENT

8060 Melrose Ave.
Suite 400
Los Angeles, CA 90046
(323) 852-1776

MARIANNE GOLAN MANAGEMENT

6528 W. 6th St.
Los Angeles, CA 90048
(323) 653-1232
mgmgmt@aol.com

MARILYN ATLAS MANAGEMENT

8899 Beverly Blvd.
Suite 704
Los Angeles, CA 90048
(310) 278-5047

MARION ROSENBERG MANAGEMENT

PO Box 69826
Los Angeles, CA 90069
(323) 653-7383
marion@marionrosenberg.com

MARTIN WEISS MANAGEMENT

PO Box 5856
Santa Monica, CA 90409
(310) 399-7658
www.mwmtalent.com

MARV DAUER & ASSOCIATES

11601 San Vicente Blvd.
Suite 104
Los Angeles, CA 90049
(310) 207-6884

MATT SHERMAN MANAGEMENT

9107 Wilshire Blvd.
Suite 225
Beverly Hills, CA 90210
(323) 465-0300
mattshermanmgt@earthlink.net

MC TALENT

4821 Lankershim Blvd.
Suite F, PMB 329
North Hollywood, CA 91601
(818) 487-8781

MCGOWAN MANAGEMENT

8733 W. Sunset Blvd.
Suite 103
West Hollywood, CA 90069
(310) 289-9157

MEGHAN SCHUMACHER MANAGEMENT

13551-D Riverside Dr., #387
Sherman Oaks, CA 91423
(818) 788-4025
meghan@meghans.net

MICHAEL LEVINE MANAGEMENT

9028 W. Sunset Blvd.
Penthouse One
Los Angeles, CA 90069
(310) 275-0875

MIDWEST TALENT MANAGEMENT

4821 Lankershim Blvd.
Suite F 149
North Hollywood, CA 91601
(818) 765-3785
www.midwesttalent.com

MILLER & COMPANY

(310) 550-0826

NEBULA MANAGEMENT

PO Box 292490
Los Angeles, CA 90029
(323) 664-8244
www.nebulamanagement.com

NIAD MANAGEMENT

15030 Ventura Blvd.
Building 19
Sherman Oaks, CA 91403
(818) 774-0051
www.niadmanagement.com

OPEN DOOR MANAGEMENT

865 Via de la Paz
Pacific Palisades, CA 90272
(310) 459-2559
www.opendoormanagement.
com

PALLAS MANAGEMENT

12535 Chandler Blvd.
Suite 1
Valley Village, CA 91607
(818) 506-8368
laurapallas@sbcglobal.net

**PATRICK RAINS AND
ASSOCIATES**

(212) 860-3233
www.prarecords.com

PAUL CANTOR ENTERPRISES

(949) 240-4400

PETER GIAGNI MANAGEMENT

8981 Sunset Blvd.
Suite 103
West Hollywood, CA 90069
(310) 246-1594
pgmgmt1@aol.com

PINE RIVER ENTERTAINMENT

1200 South Corning St.
Suite 101
Los Angeles, CA 90036
(310) 659-1039
pinevrmgt@aol.com

PRECISION ENTERTAINMENT

6338 Wilshire Blvd.
Los Angeles, CA 90048
(323) 692-9214
www.precisionentertainment
groupinc.com

PRINCIPAL ENTERTAINMENT

1964 Westwood Blvd.
Suite 400
Los Angeles, CA 90025
(310) 446-1466
www.principalent.net

PRINCIPATO YOUNG

9465 Wilshire Blvd.
Suite 880
Beverly Hills, CA 90212
(310) 274-4474

PROTÉGÉ ENTERTAINMENT

710 E. Angeleno Ave.
Burbank, CA 91501
(818) 842-2000
protegemgt@aol.com

RAIN MANAGEMENT GROUP

12300 Wilshire Blvd.
Suite 425
Los Angeles, CA 91604
(310) 481-9800

RITA B. MANAGEMENT

4624 Cahuenga Blvd.
Suite 205
Toluca Lake, CA 91602
(310) 902-3363
www.ritabmanagement.com

ROBIN BROOKS TALENT MANAGEMENT

5619 Lankershim Blvd.
Suite 1104
North Hollywood, CA 91601
(949) 460-0858
robinbrooksmngt@aol.com

RUGOLO ENTERTAINMENT

195 S. Beverly Dr., #400
Beverly Hills, CA 90212
(310) 550-1124
gina@rugoloentertainment.com

SAGER MANAGEMENT

260 S. Beverly Dr.
Beverly Hills, CA 90212
(310) 274-4555

SANDERS·ARMSTRONG MANAGEMENT

2120 Colorado Blvd.
Suite 120
Santa Monica, CA 90404
(310) 315-2100

SHALLON STAR MANAGEMENT GROUP

14320 Ventura Blvd.
Suite 624
Sherman Oaks, CA 91423
(818) 990-9881
shallonstar@sbcglobal.net

SHARP TALENT

117 North Orlando Ave.
Los Angeles, CA 90048
(323) 653-4104
sharptalent@ca.rr.com

SHARYN TALENT MANAGEMENT

PO Box 18033
Encino, CA 91416
(818) 609-7463
sharyntalent@mac.com

SNEAK PREVIEW ENTERTAINMENT

6705 Sunset Blvd.
2nd Floor
Hollywood, CA 90028
(323) 962-0295
www.sneakpreview
entertain.com

STEIN ENTERTAINMENT

1351 N. Crescent Heights
Blvd., #312
West Hollywood, CA 90046
(323) 822-1400
www.steinentertainment.com

SUCHIN COMPANY, THE

PO Box 570523
Tarzana, CA 91356
(818) 344-0600

SUSAN OSSER TALENT COMPANY

(818) 994-9123
susanossertalent@aol.com

SWEENEY MANAGEMENT

8755 Lookout Mountain Ave.
Los Angeles, CA 90046
(323) 822-3000

THIRDHILL ENTERTAINMENT

195 S. Beverly Dr.
Suite 400
Beverly Hills, CA 90212
(310) 786-1936
thirdhill@thirdhill
entertainment.com

TRADEMARK TALENT

4758 Allott Ave.
Sherman Oaks, CA 91423
(818) 905-8899
www.trademarktalent.com

TRUVISION ENTERTAINMENT

11516 Moorpark St.
Suite 3
Studio City, CA 91602
(818) 536-3410
truvision@pacbell.net

UNTITLED ENTERTAINMENT

1801 Century Park East
Suite 700
Los Angeles, CA 90067
(310) 601-2100

**WHITAKER
ENTERTAINMENT**

4924 Vineland Ave.
North Hollywood, CA 91601
(818) 766-4441
whitakerentertainment.com

WILLIAMS UNLIMITED

5010 Buffalo Ave.
Sherman Oaks, CA 91423
(818) 905-1058
www.williamsunltd.com

**YES DEAR
ENTERTAINMENT**

(310) 481-2020
www.yesdearent.com

GLOSSARY

AFTRA

the American Federation of Television and Radio Artists (AFTRA), a national labor union that represents performers, journalists, and other artists in the entertainment and broadcast media.

AGENT

a handler who represents talent, whose primary function is to secure work for his or her clients.

ART DEPARTMENT

the department that executes the vision of the production designer in creating the look of the film.

ASSISTANT DIRECTOR

the crew member responsible for delegating the director's instructions and making sure the cast and crew are in their required positions at the right time.

AUDITION

a meeting that is held between a casting director and an actor whereby the actor can demonstrate his talent and the casting director can gauge if that actor is right for a role.

AVAIL

"on avail"—a designation for an actor who is being considered for a role. An actor on avail must notify the production if another offer comes in.

BACKGROUND

see Extra.

BOOKING

term used when an actor is hired for a role.

BREAKDOWNS

casting notices.

BUSINESS AFFAIRS

a studio or agency department, generally run by attorneys, that negotiates contracts.

CALL SHEET

daily report that lists the time the cast and crew are to arrive on set.

CALL TIME

the time the cast and crew are to arrive on set.

CALLBACK

a subsequent audition for an actor being considered for a role in a theater, film, or TV project.

CASTING ASSISTANT

the casting director's assistant, whose primary responsibility is to answer the phone and schedule auditions.

CASTING ASSOCIATE

the casting director's right-hand man, who helps set up and even run some casting sessions.

CASTING DIRECTOR

the person responsible for selecting lead and supporting actors for a film or television show.

CASTING EXECUTIVE

an executive on the studio or network level who supervises the casting of all projects at the studio or network.

COMMUNITY THEATER

local theater groups throughout the country that hold open calls where anyone can audition.

COMP CARDS

used primarily in the fashion industry, a compilation of shots showing a model in different looks and styles.

COSTAR

television term that describes a small guest role on a TV show.

COMMERCIAL AGENT

an agent who represents talent for on-camera commercials.

COOGAN ACCOUNT

a blocked trust account that is required to get a work permit.

CRAFT SERVICES

crew members responsible for feeding the cast and crew between meals on set.

DEAL MEMO

an abbreviated agreement outlining the major terms of a deal prior to a long-form contract.

DEVELOPMENT EXECUTIVE

a studio or network executive who finds and develops new projects.

DIRECTOR

the primary creative and artistic force behind a film; in charge of the actors' performances on camera and determining the overall look and feel of the film.

DOUBLE BANGER

a trailer with two dressing rooms, one for each actor.

EPISODIC

a television series that consists of multiple episodes.

EQUITY

Actors Equity Association (AEA), a labor union that represents actors and stage managers in professional theater.

EXTRA

a background actor who does not have any lines.

FEATURE

a motion picture, or film.

FILM COMMISSION

city, state, or country office set up to entice filming in its community and to assist in filming activity within that community.

FITTING

an opportunity for an actor to try on his costume prior to shooting so that alterations can be made.

GENERAL MEETING

a meeting for a casting director to get to know an actor better.

GO-SEE

a print audition.

GUEST STAR

a large guest role on a TV show.

HEADSHOT

an actor's business card—typically eight inches wide by ten inches long—which shows a picture of the actor and is sent to casting offices for the purpose of securing auditions.

HONEY WAGON

the smallest-sized trailer, lacking any frills.

LOCAL HIRE

an actor who is hired locally, thereby eliminating travel, housing, or per diem costs for the production.

MAIN TITLES

the credit sequence that appears at the beginning of a film or TV show, or, in cases where there are no credits at the beginning of a film, the credit sequence that immediately follows a movie.

MANAGER

a talent rep whose primary function is to guide and advise an actor's career.

MEAL PENALTY

a fine imposed on a production if a meal isn't served within six hours of call time or from the previous meal.

NETWORK (V)

to make contacts in the industry that will be beneficial to launching or helping your career.

NON-UNION

an actor who is not a member of SAG, AFTRA, or Equity.

OFF-BOOK

when an actor does not need to rely on his sides for an audition.

PER DIEM

spending money to cover actors' incidental expenses while filming on location.

PHOTO DOUBLE

See Stand-in.

PLUS TEN

an agent's commission that is often negotiated into scale deals so that the actor doesn't have to deduct that commission from his salary.

PREPRODUCTION

everything that takes place before filming commences.

PRE-READ

the very first audition with a casting director.

PRODUCER

the person who is ultimately responsible for the success or failure of a film, and the person who generally oversees a project from initial concept through release. In television, the producers are the writers who ultimately guide the creative vision of the series.

PRODUCTION

general term used to describe the filming of a movie or TV show.

PROGRAMMING EXECUTIVE

studio or network executive who supervises current television programs.

PUBLICIST

a handler whose primary job is to generate press and media coverage for an actor.

READER

the person in an audition who reads lines opposite the performer who is auditioning.

REEL

a visual resume used by actors to show a sample of their work.

REGIONAL THEATERS

professional theater companies throughout the country that produce their own seasons.

RESIDUALS

payments made to a performer for subsequent screenings of their work.

SAG

Screen Actors Guild (SAG), a national labor union that represents actors for film and television.

SCALE

minimum payment for an actor, pre-negotiated by the unions.

SERIES REGULAR

an actor who is part of the main cast of a television series.

SIDES

audition copy.

STAND-IN

a person, other than the actor, who is used to block and light a scene that involves that actor.

STAR WAGON

the largest dressing room available to an actor while shooting on location.

STUDIO TEACHER

a certified teacher who teaches on a set and also looks out for the safety and welfare of child actors.

TABLE READ

when the entire cast of actors reads the script out loud, enabling the writers and producers to hear how their words sound so that changes can be made if necessary.

TAFT-HARTLEY

the process by which a non-union actor is given a line in a film or TV show, thereby making him or her eligible to join the union.

TEST

an audition before studio and/or network executives.

TEST DEAL

a pre-negotiated agreement that is set prior to an actor testing for a film or TV series.

THEATRICAL AGENT

an agent who represents talent for film and television.

THRESHOLD SKILLS

a special skill set that combines confidence and personality, necessary for when an actor first walks into a room.

TOP OF SHOW

the largest guest star role on an episodic television show.

TRIPLE BANGER

a trailer with three dressing rooms, one for each actor.

TURNAROUND TIME

the period between when a production wraps and when they begin again the next day. Actors must be given at least twelve hours of turnaround time.

VOICE-OVER AGENT

an agent who represents talent for radio ads and animation.

WARDROBE

a meeting with the costume department, generally to get measurements taken or to try on clothes.

WORK PERMIT

a legal document that allows children to work in the entertainment industry.

WORK SESSION

an opportunity for an actor to work one-on-one with a director or casting director before an audition or test.

YOUTH MARKET

any actor under eighteen, or an actor over eighteen who plays under eighteen.

ZED CARD

See Comp card.

ABOUT THE AUTHOR

FREDERICK LEVY is the author of several books about the entertainment industry, including *Hollywood 101: The Film Industry*, *Short Films 101: How to Make a Short and Launch Your Filmmaking Career*, and *15 Minutes of Fame: Becoming a Star in the YouTube Revolution*. This is his sixth book.

Levy is the owner of Management 101, a firm that guides the careers of actors, authors, screenwriters, and music acts. He is also a partner of the Levy Leder Company, a firm that develops and produces film and television shows. On the production side, Frederick is the co-creator and executive producer of *Dance on Sunset* for Nickelodeon. He was an executive producer on the feature film *Unknown* starring Jim Caviezel and Greg Kinnear, for the Weinstein Company, as well as a producer on *Frailty*, starring Bill Paxton and Matthew McConaughey, for Lions Gate Films.

Levy can be reached through his website at www.fredericklevy.com, his YouTube Channel at www.YouTube.com/FrederickLevy, or through his Facebook fan page.

INDEX

S